Praise for The Essential Associate

"Jay has been there, done it, and learned from it. His gift is succinctly communicating his and others' lessons learned. An enjoyable read that will help you succeed."

Scott Wolfson, Partner at Wolfson Bolton

"Making the transition from legal philosopher (law school) to legal practitioner is the hardest step every lawyer must make. *The Essential Associate* is a vital resource to facilitate that process."

Paul H. Burton, Founder QuietSpacing, LLC

"If you're a new associate looking for fundamental advice on how to get ahead, *The Essential Associate* is a great place to start."

Keith Lee, Attorney, Author, and Founder of Associate's Mind and LawyerSmack

"*The Essential Associate* is a must-read for anyone starting a legal career or hoping to take their career to the next level. It's highly practical, and brimming with concrete advice from high-performing law firm partners on the qualities they are looking for in young lawyers. The first step to a successful legal career is graduating from law school. The next is reading *The Essential Associate*."

Felicia Perlman, Partner at Skadden, Arps, Slate, Meagher & Flom

JAY HARRINGTON

THE
ESSENTIAL
ASSOCIATE

Step up, stand out, and rise
to the top as a young lawyer

ORDERING INFORMATION

For additional copies visit www.TheEssentialAssociate.com, www.attorneyatwork.com/books, or www.amazon.com. Quantity discounts available—for more information visit www.TheEssentialAssociate.com or email the author at jay@hcommunications.biz.

ISBN
978-0-9995545-2-4

For more information and free resources related to the book, visit **www.TheEssentialAssociate.com.**

TABLE OF CONTENTS

PART ONE: STEP UP
EXCEL AT THE PRACTICE OF LAW

PART TWO: STAND OUT
EXCEL IN THE BUSINESS OF LAW

Introduction

"A pessimist sees the difficulty in every opportunity;
an optimist sees the opportunity in every difficulty."
— WINSTON CHURCHILL

T oward the tail-end of my first year as an associate, a partner walked up to me at the firm's holiday party and said, "You're famous!" He had a hint of a smile but a steely look in his eyes. I focused on the eyes because I knew exactly what he was referring to. It wasn't good.

Earlier that day, a pleading peppered with my name and appended with a bunch of emails that I wrote was filed in a multi-billion dollar Chapter 11 bankruptcy case by an adverse party. At issue was a "he said/he said" situation in which opposing counsel acknowledged missing a critical deadline related to a multi-million dollar claim against my client but was making the case that I had consented to a late-filed claim. I had not, but after reading through his pleading I realized that I was sloppy in my communications. I had opened the door just enough for him to point his finger back at me.

If you're a first-year associate at a big law firm, there is virtually zero chance that becoming "famous" for something you do at work is a good thing. And while the partner's use of the term was obviously sarcastic, I was experiencing my first "15 minutes of fame" (more like notoriety) within the halls of my law firm.

It was a tight spot. Because I had been doing reliable work on the case I was taking on more responsibility with less oversight. But I was still playing a supporting role and this was the first time I had the spotlight on me for something I did wrong. I had a choice: I could either own the problem and fix it or shrink from it and let someone else deal with it. It wasn't easy, and I ended up with a bruised ego, but by tackling the issue head-on with the help of my colleagues the issue got resolved. I became a better lawyer by learning from the experience.

The odds are that you've experienced something similar or soon will. These are the type of moments that determine the trajectory of your career. It may be a positive moment or a negative one. Sometimes circumstances like this result from actions you take or fail to take. Other times they're due to conditions outside of your control but you have to confront them nonetheless. If a lawyer's life was depicted in a movie, this type of moment would be called an "inciting incident."

In screenplay and novel writing the inciting incident is the event that gets the story rolling. It's the action or decision that introduces the problem that the story's main character must overcome. In *Jerry Maguire*, it's the moment that Jerry writes his manifesto about the need to put people first in the sports agency business. It leads to his firing and he walks away from his power job to start over.

In movies and books the inciting incident is unmistakable. It's the moment that calls the protagonist to action and changes their life irrevocably. That's the thing about fiction—almost every story follows the same arc. There's background, struggle, and ultimately triumph, with twists and turns along the way. But the story almost always gets resolved, wrapped up in a pretty bow. More often than not the protagonist lives happily ever after, having defeated the villain, gotten the girl, or defused the bomb, just in the nick of time.

Art may imitate life, but real life is, of course, far different. And messier (at least the ending). We're all characters in a narrative, but unlike in most books and movies our stories don't always result in happy endings. Inciting incidents occur all around us but rarely do they lead to real change. Often we miss their meaning altogether. Other times we recognize their significance but we are unable or unwilling to leverage their transformational power. We have a health scare but do little to improve our lifestyle. We struggle at work but instead of taking the time to understand the cause of our struggles, we plow forward with no real plan to make the future different than the past.

The same is true of organizations and entire industries. It's hard to believe that the buggy whip industry missed the automotive revolution; typewriter makers didn't see the power of personal computers; the taxi industry overlooked what Uber and Lyft saw; and the music industry didn't adapt to the digitization of its product. How did the retail sector not see Amazon coming? Why didn't hotels crush Airbnb when they had the chance? It happens over and over. In every industry, market participants miss (or completely ignore) inciting incidents that should lead to transformational change. They remain stagnant, unable or unwilling to fundamentally change behaviors that could lead to a change in fortunes. Their marketplaces disintermediate and they're left scrambling to catch up.

What does this have to do with achieving success as a law firm associate? As someone who is operating in today's legal industry you don't have the luxury of ambivalence to the winds of change swirling around you. Your employer is buffeting against these forces and you must too. There's little chance that today's law firms will go the way of early twentieth-century buggy whip makers. But inciting incidents, beckoning lawyers and law firms to change, are happening more frequently as the broader economy continues the transformation from the industrial age to the information age.

Since last decade's Great Recession there has been a fundamental change in the legal landscape. Much like what happened to the housing market before last decade's meltdown in the financial markets, the legal marketplace has shifted from a seller's to a buyer's market.

This has led to downward pressure on fees, increased demand for alternative billing practices, and more significant competition for fewer opportunities. Law firms continue to consolidate in an attempt to achieve economies of scale. Work has also moved in-house as corporate law departments have looked for ways to cut costs and figure out more efficient models and methods of acquiring the legal services.

The "2018 Report on the State of the Legal Market" (the "Report"), published by Georgetown University Law Center and Thomson Reuters Legal Executive Institute, highlights these trends and punctuates the need for change. According to the Report, there is flat demand for law firm services despite growing demand for legal services; less leverage (fewer associates per partner) at law firms; weakening collections; falling productivity; rising competition; a lack of innovation among law firms even though clients are demanding more of it; and loss of law firm market share to alternative service providers. The Report suggests that too many firms are fighting the "last war" by making changes based on how the market has behaved in the past and not on what's to come.

Entrepreneurs have eagerly stepped in to fill in the gaps. From overseas document review firms to Silicon Valley technology start-ups, alternative service providers continue to chip away at work that traditionally was within the exclusive domain of lawyers and law firms. Companies such as LegalZoom and Rocket Lawyer, which were once seen as novelties, continue to gain ground. Big Four accounting firms are building their own legal services departments around the world. Some are as big as the largest global law firms.

Headlines in legal tech publications trumpet the inevitable march of artificial intelligence in the legal industry, and its power to displace and disrupt many of the essential functions provided by today's lawyers and law firms. Some speculate that blockchain technology (the foundational technology of cryptocurrencies such as Bitcoin), will obviate the need for "middlemen" such as lawyers, and even judges, when it comes to negotiating, performing, and enforcing rights and obligations related to transactions. Depending on who you believe, this is just the tip of the blockchain iceberg.

The struggles of many firms in this no-growth market shouldn't come as a huge surprise. Despite the challenges, it's business as usual in many quarters. Law firms like Sedgwick, Howrey, Burleson, Dewey & LeBoeuf, and other venerable brand names have shuttered in recent years. Others are consolidating to survive.

There will come a time, as you progress in your career and become a law firm leader, that you will be in a position to directly address and influence the broader issues facing the legal industry. But for now, as a young associate, the primary challenge you face is putting yourself in a position to not just survive but thrive in today's law firm environment. By doing so, you'll not only experience success but also lift up those around you through your actions.

Newton's second law of inertia states that an object at rest will remain at rest unless acted upon by an outside force. Take a hard look around. Outside forces are gathering and calling you to action. The question is: In the face of these challenges, will you lean in or look the other way?

The fact that you're reading this book suggests that you're someone who doesn't shrink in the face of a challenge and is motivated to learn, grow, and take charge of your career. That's great, because while periods of change pose lots of obstacles, they also present massive opportunities.

To borrow a phrase from Dickens, for young lawyers in today's legal market, it's both the best of times and the worst of times. "Worst of times" because there's no place to hide. Clients are less willing to pay for young associate time (what some clients perceive as "on the job training"). Law firms can't afford to put up with mediocre performance. Firms are expecting more value from their associates because clients are expecting more from them.

Things are changing so fast that young associates today face challenges that others before them did not. There was comfort in being told, during the "good old days," that you just needed to keep your head down and do good work and everything else would fall into place in due time. There was a sense of relief in thinking that there was plenty of business to go around for talented lawyers, so there was no need to worry about business development. In today's environment, any comfort derived from such advice is false.

On the other hand, these are the "best of times" because it's during moments like these, when things get tough, that merit matters most and there are opportunities to achieve stand-out success. Young lawyers today have the chance to achieve things that were never before possible. The Internet has changed everything. There are fewer gatekeepers and those that remain have less influence. A small firm, small market, entrepreneurial-minded young lawyer can leave just as big of a footprint in the digital landscape as anyone else.

Want to make a significant impact as a young associate? There's little to stop you, no matter who you are or where you are, except for your own limiting beliefs about what's possible.

Don't you want to see what you're capable of? It's time to step up to the challenge and stand out among your peers.

WHO THIS BOOK IS FOR

I've been competing in the legal industry for close to twenty years, first as a lawyer and now as an executive coach and consultant, and there have been lots of ups and downs in the market during this time period. I began my career as a corporate bankruptcy associate at Skadden, Arps, Slate, Meagher & Flom one week after the 9/11 terrorist attacks. I co-founded a law firm in early 2009 in Detroit at the height of the financial crisis. For over a decade, I have been coaching and consulting with top lawyers and law firms who are navigating the same choppy waters that you're now swimming in. I've learned through these experiences what it takes to succeed as a law firm associate in good times and bad.

Some of the most valuable lessons come from the time I spent at my own small firm. I achieved success, but it was neither the clients nor the financial rewards that made a lasting impact. Indeed, those things were fleeting. What mattered most was that through this experience I learned what it's like to have real agency and ownership over my legal career. It wasn't that working at my small firm, as opposed to a "Biglaw" firm, was easier or more exciting. In many respects running a small law firm is far harder and more stressful than working at a big one. What made the greatest difference was that, through the entrepreneurial experience of founding and running my own firm, I finally learned what it takes to master both the practice of law and the business of law. Up to that point I had focused almost exclusively on the former.

The practice of law still wasn't fun. What job is? For the first time, however, it was deeply satisfying. I learned that while the work, itself, may not bring joy, it is possible to learn to love the "fruits," including the personal growth and professional satisfaction, of my labor.

The problem is that many lawyers only learn these lessons (if at all) in hindsight. I wrote this book so that you don't have to.

With that said, this book is not for everyone. It's not even for every young lawyer. I wrote it for young lawyers who aspire to succeed, grow, and advance on a partnership track at a law firm (or at least want to keep the partnership option open). Are you hoping to succeed in a law firm environment? If so continue reading.

At the same time, let's face facts: You have a tough road ahead of you. The path to partnership is becoming increasingly treacherous. The number of equity partners at law firms has increased at a relatively slow pace over the past fifteen years while the overall number of attorneys has surged. The combination of fewer equity partners, more competition among firms, and more lawyers in the system means that associates who hope to make partner face increasingly difficult odds.

The reason it's important to know what path you're on, or at least want to be on, is that advancing in a law firm requires a unique skill set. To succeed in a legal career outside of a law firm you need to be an excellent lawyer. To become successful in a law firm, you need to be an excellent lawyer and also generate work for yourself and others.

A law firm partner has two jobs: producing excellent work product and building a book of business. The reason it's difficult to make partner is that the skills required to become both an excellent lawyer and adept at developing business are difficult ones to master. They're valuable skills because they're in short supply. As a result, most lawyers who are up for partner go into the process with little confidence about the outcome.

It's not that these lawyers haven't excelled at what they do. In order to even be considered for partner at a law firm it means that a lawyer: (1) has worked really hard, racked up big billable hours, and as a result has contributed greatly to the firm's bottom-line; (2) possesses expertise or a unique skill that the firm values (an IP lawyer with a Ph.D. in computer science, for example); or (3) has demonstrated the ability to generate significant business. However, it's rare for an associate to batch these skills and qualities together. As a result, most associates wait with baited breath and fingers crossed to learn their fate.

But note that I said "most." There are always a few who figure out the system and learn what it takes to make partner. These are the associates for whom the partnership vote is not a cliffhanger but a foregone conclusion. Why? They've managed to become so valuable that they've flipped the balance of power. Because they're so valuable, they have the leverage in decisions related to their career advancement, not their firms. Firms are so concerned about losing these lawyers to competitors that they have no choice but to make them a partner.

An associate with leverage is one who has gained mastery of both the practice of law and the business of law; one who acts like an entrepreneur and not an employee; one who recognizes that their potential is limitless and that they can generate significant value for their clients and their firm at any stage of their career. Because it's rare to find associates like this, they are essential in the sense that they stand out among their colleagues for all the right reasons. If someone is essential, it means others perceive them as absolutely necessary. In today's market, to be considered for partner, you need to be an "Essential Associate."

Essential Associate

Practice of Law • Business of Law

Building mastery as a lawyer and building a book of business both take a long time. You can't focus on one or the other in isolation. There's an old Russian proverb that states: "If you chase two rabbits you will not catch either one." But when it comes to focusing on the dual priorities required for advancement in a law firm, you have no choice but to be smart and agile enough to work intensely on both at the same time.

PUTTING THE IDEAS FROM THIS BOOK INTO ACTION

In the coming chapters of this book, we'll go deep into strategies and tactics related to what it takes to become an Essential Associate at a law firm. In Part One, we'll address what's necessary to become a lawyer capable of producing outstanding work product and delivering impeccable client service (i.e., the practice of law). Part Two focuses on the essential actions required to lay the foundation for future business development (i.e., the business of law).

But first, let's discuss how to make the ideas in this book serve as more than mere inspiration. After all, it's easy to read a book, feel motivated, put the book down, and then move on, without doing anything to put the ideas from the book into action. Time spent learning is wasted if not paired with action.

As a young lawyer, it's easy to overlook a lurking risk: You have a long time to do what it takes to become an Essential Associate. Because you have time it's easy to do nothing. Procrastination and complacency are two of the most significant threats to your success. It's far easier to react to the urgency of the day-to-day than it is to plan strategically for the next year—or eight years—of your career. But if you want to make partner this is the type of long-term thinking that is required. Start today because eight years will go by faster than you think.

Learning the Essential Associate principles is an excellent first step. The next one involves implementing them over time as part of your daily routine. The best way to do this, as we'll now address, is to: (1) think big, (2) establish priorities, and (3) act small. Think of this book as a road map for a long journey ahead. The only way you'll get to your destination is one step at a time.

Think Big

Thinking big is expansive thinking. Thinking small is restrictive thinking. Thinking big is all about possibilities. Thinking small is all about limitations. Have big dreams? You need to think big. The odds of making partner at a law firm are stacked against you, so to make your big dream become a reality you need to set equally big goals for yourself.

Many people confuse dreams and goals. A dream is loose and

ephemeral. It's important to have dreams, but it's easy to dismiss a dream as out of reach. That's because there's often a big gap between a dream and our belief about what's possible. You can only realize a dream by creating a goal associated with it and then pursuing the goal by taking action.

Elon Musk dreamed about making it big in the United States when he emigrated to Canada from South Africa at the age of seventeen, but his vision of bringing electric cars (and ultimately space travel) to mass markets would have remained just a dream had he not backed it up with strategic thinking and tireless action. The same process is required to realize your dream of making partner at a law firm.

A concrete goal requires us to think more deeply about what we want and commit to a series of specific actions that will get us there. A dream is focused on outcomes. A goal is focused on actions. A dream is what you want. A goal is how you get there. A goal, like a dream, is about reaching a destination, but setting a goal requires far more planning for the journey.

A goal requires systems, processes, metrics, start dates, and deadlines. There's a saying that "if you dream it, you can do it," but too often we don't. A simple shift in thinking, which allows us to think in terms of goals and not dreams, is what leads us to roll up our sleeves, get to work, and move forward. You can't think small and short-term if you want to achieve big things over the long-term.

Accordingly, don't just dream about making partner at a law firm, make it a concrete goal. Given the odds it's an audacious one. But that's good. The best goals are big ones.

Set Priorities

Once you've established a big goal for yourself—in this case, making partner at a law firm—the next step in the process is setting priorities that will help you to achieve it. There are many actions you can take to reach your goal. The challenge lies in prioritizing the activities that produce the most significant impact. It's not enough to merely identify your goals; you must ensure that your goals guide your everyday actions.

In his book, *Tools of Titans*, Tim Ferriss writes that in recent years he has started to regularly ask himself a question that helps him to maintain a long-term focus on his most important goals, and commit to everyday action to achieve them. The question is, "Am I hunting antelopes or field mice?"

The premise of the "antelopes and field mice" question is as follows: A lion is capable of hunting and eating field mice if it wants to, but the energy required to catch a field mouse exceeds its potential nourishment. If a lion spends its days chasing mice, it will slowly starve to death.

Instead, lions must hunt antelopes, which are big and nourishing. An antelope requires more effort to hunt. But once captured it provides ample fuel for a long happy life.

As lawyers, "field mice" fill our days. We focus on short-term goals. There's always endless busy work to do. We react to the urgent and put off the important. When it comes to critical priorities such as marketing and business development, we fit in what we can when we can. Many of the activities we engage in result in little impact and are disconnected from any broader strategy. They might provide a momentary sense of pleasure or satisfaction but don't serve a long-term purpose. In other words, we hunt field mice.

Successful lawyers hunt antelopes. "Antelopes" include things like cultivating and maintaining relationships, developing real skills and unique expertise, tackling high impact projects, and contributing to something greater than ourselves. These activities make our lives and careers meaningful. They take time and effort to accomplish, but in the end the payoff is significant.

Becoming an Essential Associate is not easy. It takes hard work and patience. But over time, through grit, resilience, and setting the right priorities for yourself, you can position yourself to achieve big things.

Once you've set a goal and established priorities, only one more crucial ingredient is required: small, incremental, everyday action.

Act Small

While thinking big is critical to becoming an Essential Associate, big things happen through consistent small actions. How do you eat an elephant (or an antelope)? As the old saying goes, it's one bite at a time.

Mark Zuckerberg might have been relegated to a footnote in business school textbooks if his goal was limited to making Facebook a Harvard-based platform. He had to dream big and set big goals to make his business a multi-billion dollar platform used by billions of people throughout the world. But he also had to go about it through a series of practical, achievable, momentum-inducing small actions. Incremental daily progress led to the news feed, status update, like button, mobile app, and ad product features that drive Facebook's growth. These features, created slowly over time, fueled Zuckerberg's big dream and transformed his ambition into reality.

The same goes for Jeff Bezos. He knew Amazon would be big, and had a plan for its growth from day one, but few others shared his vision. Bezos had to start very small by working out of his garage, fulfilling book orders one by one, until he could convince others of the Internet's potential for e-commerce.

The problem that many young lawyers face in making real progress in their careers is twofold: overwhelm and over-ambition. They feel overwhelmed by how busy they are, and do little to habitually improve their skills and lay the groundwork for future business development. Because they're not taking small steps forward every day, they try to make up for lost time by engaging in a flurry of activity later in their careers. They become over-ambitious (out of necessity) for short-term periods and burn out.

Randy Juip is a partner at Foley, Baron, Metzger & Juip. At a relatively young age, he earned a reputation as a skilled trial lawyer and developed an impressive book of business. This didn't happen by accident. Randy recognized the need to move forward on his big picture career objectives, such as developing client relationships, while dealing with the day-to-day challenges of a busy litigation practice. He kept his career and his caseload moving forward in tandem. Many young lawyers become so overwhelmed by their work that they let everything else fall by the wayside.

According to Randy, "Many associates spend all of their time putting out fires. They need to set aside time to think about and act on things like business development that are important but not urgent. It's important to always be thinking long-term. The law is a business that needs long-term strategic thinking and corresponding short-term action."

By failing to think big and act small, many young associates find themselves in a bind later on in their careers. Because they take no regular action toward their goals they're forced to play catch up. The only way to achieve what they want is to try to muscle their way there through grandiose plans they're incapable of executing. The urgency and immensity of the task before them leads to paralyzing overwhelm and corresponding inaction.

There's a better approach to success. Instead of trying to do everything all at once, focus on one thing at a time. Identify the lead domino that will help advance your career step-by-step. Success doesn't happen all at once—it's sequential.

Put another way, it's not all of the big, bold things you do that lead to success. It's the small actions taken every day that make the difference and lead to compounding results over time.

Incremental daily progress is the key to sustainable growth in life and in a legal career. Ready to get started?

PART I

STEP UP

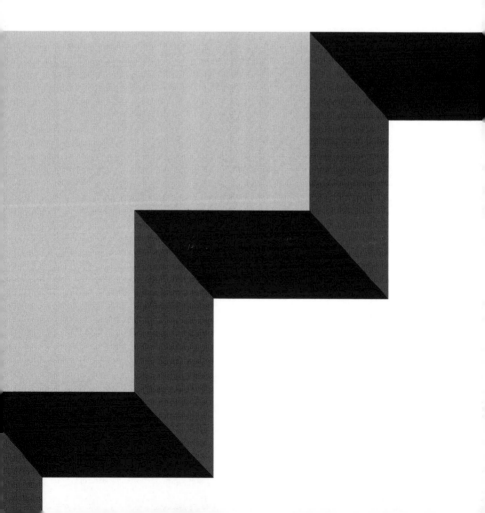

EXCEL AT THE PRACTICE
OF LAW

1

The Characteristics of an Essential Associate

"Unless you try to do something beyond what you have already mastered, you will never grow."

– RALPH WALDO EMERSON

here is not a single archetype of a successful lawyer. But there are characteristics shared by most lawyers who excel in a law firm environment. How do I know? I learned these lessons by observing what it takes to become successful at the practice of law during the course of my own legal career while working at top law firms and starting one of my own, and over the last decade through my work as an executive coach and consultant working with hundreds of lawyers and law firms. Also, through extensive research, interviews with many top lawyers, and conversations with consultants who work with lawyers, I've gathered and distilled the collective wisdom of many other experts about what it takes to shine as a young associate.

One of these experts is attorney Keith Lee of the Hamer Law Group. Keith is also an author, writes the Associate's Mind blog (one of the most popular legal blogs), and is the founder of LawyerSmack, a thriving online community for lawyers.

I spoke to Keith about what it takes to succeed as an associate and make partner at a law firm. The most important thing, Keith explained, is having the right mindset. "Before an associate can become a partner, other partners must think of the associate as a partner," Keith said.

In other words, an associate who hopes to make partner can't wait until they become a partner to start acting like one.

They must think and act like a partner, both regarding the characteristics they manifest and behaviors they exhibit, so that others who have decision-making power can envision them as a member of their ranks. According to Keith, "Young associates must demonstrate leadership by learning to delegate work and manage others, and accountability by taking ownership of problems and fixing them." As you progress in your career as an associate, you must start to act as if you are a partner if you hope to become a partner. You must start asking yourself questions such as, "What would a partner do in this situation?" More importantly, you must then act accordingly.

You'll meet more of these experts (including more from Keith) in chapters to come. They come from a variety of backgrounds. Some work at big firms, and others at small ones. Some are not lawyers at all but have worked with and trained successful lawyers for decades.

I also share the wisdom and work habits of many accomplished individuals outside of the law; people with wide-ranging experiences across different disciplines and industries, from billionaire entrepreneur Sara Blakely to J.J. Watt of the Houston Texans. This advice is buttressed by research from top academics. All have strong and sometimes varied points of view that inform what it takes to succeed in a legal career. However, after having synthesized and analyzed the data, clear patterns began to emerge about what's important. What I found is that there are five characteristics that Essential Associates embody and exhibit as they advance in their legal careers.

To become an Essential Associate, you must:

1. Take Ownership

2. Be Resilient

3. Be Productive

4. Be Growth-Minded

5. Seek Balance

Think of these "Five Characteristics" as the foundation upon which to build a legal career that is strong, satisfying, and successful. Note that the Five Characteristics don't include discrete skills such as "strong writing skills" or "ability to manage projects." These types of skills are important, but lawyers who are accountable, resilient, productive, growth-minded, and balanced tend to develop all of the discrete skills necessary to become excellent lawyers. However, those who lack the foundation of the Five Characteristics often struggle despite any other discrete abilities they may possess.

The good news is that the Five Characteristics are not innate traits; they can be learned, strengthened, and cultivated over time. For example, you may not consider yourself to be particularly resilient at the moment, but you can learn to become more resilient. Part One of this book is a distillation of the way that Essential Associates think, act, and carry themselves as they progress in their careers.

Much of what must be learned to become an Essential Associate is only discernible through struggles and mistakes. Growth will come slowly, which is why patience and a long-term perspective are required. You may be feeling disheartened because the passion you thought you had for the practice of law is waning as the realities of the challenging career you've chosen are setting in.

Keep moving forward.

As you'll learn in the pages ahead, you may not be passionate about your job now, but as you improve your skills and your autonomy grows, your passion for the practice of law will grow as well. Just stay confident and put in the hard work required to get to the other side where greater rewards await.

There are no shortcuts. If you want to become an Essential Associate you need to be in this for the long haul. In fact, a long-term view can be one of your most significant competitive advantages as a young lawyer because so few people have one.

In this sense, success is like an iceberg. Only a small tip of an iceberg is visible above water but a mass of ice lies hidden below the surface. The same is true of success. It's easy to recognize an outcome but not always the hard work and dedication required to achieve it. The work you put in now, which may feel like thankless drudgery at times, will pay valuable dividends down the road. Step up and get started now, but don't expect everything to happen all at once. It's the consistency, not necessarily the intensity, of your effort that will make all of the difference.

2

Take Ownership

"We are made wise not by the recollection of our
past, but by the responsibility for our future."

– GEORGE BERNARD SHAW

Your law firm cares about your personal and professional growth. But make no mistake, the law is a business and an ultra-competitive one at that. Your firm has made a major investment in you regarding your salary, benefits, training, and overhead. It expects a return on that investment. As a young lawyer, it's important to understand your firm's point of view about the value, or lack thereof, that you contribute to the firm's overall success, and to a high degree it comes down to dollars and cents.

Foley, Baron, Metzger & Juip partner Clyde Metzger believes that too few associates understand and appreciate how law firm leaders evaluate associates' contributions to a firm's bottom-line. According to Clyde, "It's difficult, but necessary, for young attorneys to understand that their time is, literally, money. They need to develop a billing skill set early on, because if they're not getting their time down on a billing statement, then it looks like they're not working." Many things contribute to an associate's overall success, but generating a positive return on investment for the firm is high on the list.

Law firms rely on leverage, which means having lots of associates in place to work and bill. Young associates are typically less valuable (in terms of dollars and cents) to their firms than mid-level and senior associates. It's a fact of life in today's economic environment that clients are less willing to subsidize the on-the-job training of young lawyers by paying for what many perceive to be unproductive time. This means that you must be productive and effective—and not just busy—to stand out.

Generate a positive return on the firm's investment year after year, and all else being equal you'll do fine. Fail to make the firm money? That's when you'll start hearing terms such as "alternate career path" and "lack of long-term career viability" during annual reviews.

But there's some critical nuance baked into this issue. Generating a positive financial return on investment is in many ways table stakes for an associate with ambitious career aspirations. You need to make money but you also need to make life easier for those around you. You've heard it before and it's true: As a young associate, you need to invest in making the partners you work for look good, which means treating them as you would a client.

> "Young lawyers must understand that their client is their assigning attorney. To stand out, make partners look good to their clients. Be prepared. Do work that no one else in your firm can do. Do what is

asked of you, but when appropriate dig deeper. Use discretion and judgment to understand what is important and what is not."

– RANDY JUIP, PARTNER AT FOLEY, BARON, METZGER & JUIP

Unfortunately, many associates learn this lesson the hard way. When I was a first-year associate, I was tasked with the unglamorous job of preparing binders for monthly omnibus court hearings scheduled for a Chapter 11 bankruptcy case. This meant having all of the pleadings, proposed orders, proffers of testimony, and exhibits for matters before the bankruptcy court prepared and organized for the partner handling the hearing. This may sound like grunt work, and in many ways it was. But it was also a job that was critically important to make sure that the partner I was working for was prepared and would look good in front of the judge, the client, and other attorneys who would be attending the court hearing.

In the days leading up to hearings, I'd often work late into the night to make sure that the information in the hearing binder reflected fast-moving developments in the case. The first time I had this responsibility, I worked tirelessly to make sure that I completed everything perfectly—all documents included and organized flawlessly. I placed binders on the partner's office chair before heading home to catch a few hours of sleep.

The next morning, after getting back to the office, I received an urgent email from the partner asking where the hearing binder was. I knew I left the binder on his chair, so before replying to the email I rushed up to his office to see if he, or his assistant, had simply missed or misplaced the binder. Upon seeing that the partner's office light was off, I immediately realized the mistake I had made. I had assumed that the partner was in town, and would be at the office, instead of double-checking to make sure he wasn't traveling or working off-site (which he frequently was).

The point is, taking ownership of this "grunt work" didn't merely involve making a hearing binder—that was only part of the job. To finish the job, to take ownership of it, and to make the partner look good, I needed to make sure that the binder got into his hands, which meant finding out where he was going to be the day before the hearing so I could deliver it to him.

Fortunately, he was in town, working at his apartment that morning after a late flight home the night before, so I had the binder to him within the hour. He wasn't happy, but my mistake wasn't catastrophic. I was able to bounce back and never made a similar blunder again. For subsequent hearings, I performed logistical ju-jitsu on many occasions to make sure that hearing binders were delivered to multiple locations to ensure that my superiors had the information they needed. By doing this small, seemingly insignificant task well, I began to assume increasing responsibility in the case. By demonstrating that I could handle the little things, I started taking ownership of bigger things.

Never shirk responsibility because you perceive a task as trivial or unimportant. In most cases, a great deal of thought goes into how projects get assigned as part of a broader training regimen. Even if zero consideration went into it, your firm still wants to see that you will commit to the execution of something minor or mundane. If someone can't handle the little details, why would they ever be trusted to manage the larger ones? Every assignment is an opportunity for you to learn, and for your superiors to learn more about you.

The best way to demonstrate value is to take ownership of all aspects of your work. Ownership is accountability. Adopting an ownership mindset reflects an understanding that your superiors don't want to micromanage you. They certainly don't want to hold your hand. They're busy and trying to keep their heads above water, too. They understand the challenges you're facing at this point in your career. Most are willing to help, but they expect you to take the lead on your projects and manage your career.

Felicia Gerber Perlman is a partner at Skadden, Arps, Slate, Meagher & Flom, and was one of my mentors when I joined the firm. I always admired how Felicia made time to counsel and advise the associates in our group despite her busy schedule. She was (and is) kind and thoughtful, but also no-nonsense. According to Felicia, "Those who take the initiative, who manage their futures, are the ones who succeed. It's about taking ownership. How do you do this? Go into the offices of senior lawyers and show interest in work beyond your discrete assignment. Study how they interact with clients and deal with issues over the phone. Curiosity is critical."

Perlman believes that associates who exhibit an ownership mindset are committed to following through even after they complete their task. "When you do a memo, find out what happened," Felicia said. "Was a pleading prepared? Does one need to be? Did the client see it and provide feedback? Follow up and ask these questions, and inquire if there is more work that you can do. If you read an article and it addresses an issue dealing with something that pertains to a case, send it to the partner you are working for with a note attached."

One of the most important things you can do to get noticed as an associate, to get the plum assignments, and to accelerate your career development, is to develop a reputation as the "go-to" person to get the job done. Do more than what is asked to demonstrate your interest and investment in the outcome of your work.

Any time you have an opportunity to take ownership of a problem or project you should. What follows are some ways to demonstrate accountability as a young associate.

SEE THE BIG PICTURE

A recurring frustration of senior lawyers is the failure of junior lawyers to grasp the big picture. It's common for a young lawyer to have a solid handle on their individual task, but not the broader context of the deal or litigation. Because of this, they may spend too much time researching and analyzing insignificant or ancillary issues, and too little time on core issues of significance. Without a grasp of the big picture, it's easy to miss issues altogether.

Demonstrating accountability begins at the beginning. When taking on an assignment, determine deadlines, and brief-back the assigning attorney on your understanding of the objectives to make sure you are on the same page. Review your notes immediately following the meeting and follow up as necessary. It's far better to revisit the issue right away than to spend the next two days spinning your wheels because you're uncertain of the next steps.

If necessary, reach out to the client yourself to ask questions (but exercise good judgment and understand the preferences of your client and the partner you are working for before taking this step). David Jaffe, former general counsel of Guardian Industries, which is one of America's largest privately held companies, and now principal at his firm, Jaffe Counsel, always encouraged young lawyers he worked with to reach out to him directly with questions. "Speak up when you have something to say," Jaffe advises. "Young lawyers must stay attuned to what the client is asking and this means asking questions. You need to be clear on the scope of the problem you've been asked to solve and the client's objective. If the client has a $20,000 problem and you come back with a $25,000 answer, well, that's a problem in itself."

When staffed on a new matter, immediately start thinking about

THE PRACTICE OF LAW

the big picture of the litigation or transaction as a whole, not just the issues before you. Taking ownership involves thinking beyond the task and anticipating needs. Don't work in a vacuum and wipe your hands clean once your project is complete. Outstanding associates are proactive and creative in finding additional ways to contribute value to the client and firm. Remember, your primary job as a young associate is to make the partners you're working for look good and be more effective at their jobs, and this requires having a holistic view of your work.

Let's say you're a litigation associate working on a section of an important brief. Meeting the bar would be producing an impeccable work product. Going above and beyond would involve reviewing and having a deep understanding of the rules of civil procedure that apply to the pleading, as well as anticipating any logistical issues related to service of process, well in advance of the filing deadline. Scott Wolfson, who is one of the founding partners of Wolfson Bolton, describes taking ownership as, "A lawyer who is asked to research three different causes of action, and during the process of research comes up with a fourth one to pursue." Anything you can do to demonstrate a contextualized and big picture understanding of what needs to happen next is valuable, impressive, and conveys an ownership mindset to your superiors.

> "Associates who succeed are those who have an innate willingness to take ownership and responsibility for the case. This means that when the assigning partner asks you to do X, do X and also think about Y."
>
> — JOEL APPLEBAUM, PARTNER AT CLARK HILL

It should be no surprise that clients value this type of thinking, too. David Jaffe said, "Clients prefer associates who respond quickly and thoughtfully, and who have studied and have an answer not only to the question asked, but are also able to see what's next."

When you have a solid grasp of the big picture, you'll be in a position to not just produce outstanding work product, but also impact the strategy of a case or transaction. Foley, Baron, Metzger & Juip partner Clyde Metzger believes that getting a handle on the big picture is one of the distinguishing characteristics of an Essential Associate. "What distinguishes rapid risers from others is the ability to go beyond what is assigned," Clyde said. "Look at the big picture. Look to the future and do what is necessary, and not just what is asked for."

Your senior colleagues are juggling lots of different issues and matters, and welcome thoughtful debate with, and insights from, informed, independent thinking associates. If you know what you're talking about, and have something valuable to say, speak up. You'll distinguish yourself by doing so.

ASSUME A LEADERSHIP ROLE

Most young associates perceive the early years in their careers as a time to be led. That's a mistake. When partners survey the associate landscape, they're looking for leaders not followers. They know that there are only a handful of associates in each class that will be elected to join the law firm partnership and they're looking for signs of leadership ability from day one.

Accordingly, it's never too early to distinguish yourself as a leader within your firm. As a lawyer fresh out of law school, this starts with taking ownership of your work. As you advance in your career, it means getting more deeply ingrained in your firm as well, by joining associate committees and volunteering to interview new job candidates.

Opportunities to demonstrate leadership arise in the context of day-to-day work. Ask your supervisory lawyer if you can take the lead on a particular aspect of a deal or case and explain how you're going to handle it. For example, if you're working on a litigation matter involving a motion for summary judgment and get tasked with researching case law, step up and volunteer to write a few sections of the supporting brief as well. Explain that you'd like to own responsibility for both the research and the drafting, present a plan detailing how you will proceed, and then get it done. If you're a bit further along in your career, exhibiting leadership might mean taking the deposition, cross-examining the witness, or negotiating the resolution. Whenever you're stepping up to take on a new responsibility, it should feel like a stretch because leadership almost always involves pushing past limits.

Show some initiative. Invest in the firm's future. Be valuable. Partners understand that a significant number of associates will move on from the firm for other opportunities, but to sustain the firm's future a smaller number must be advanced to assume leadership roles within the firm. Want to be considered for advancement? You need to take ownership and assume leadership roles at every stage of your career as an associate.

BE ENGAGED BY BEING PRESENT

Almost all of the successful lawyers I spoke to while conducting research for this book stressed how critical it is for young lawyers to be present and engaged within their physical work environments. You need to be a member of the team, and to be on the team you need to be physically present as much as possible. According to Wolfson Bolton partner Scott Wolfson, "Face time is critical in your first year. Young lawyers need to integrate. They need to be present to immerse themselves in the firm, its people, and its culture. There is no substitute for this."

This perception seems to be a contrarian reaction to the growing and increasingly loud chorus exhorting the value and importance of flexible and remote work environments. Remote work opportunities appeal to many young associates, and they provide flexibility and can promote efficiency, but many firm leaders believe that these benefits are outweighed by the lessons that can only be learned by being present. Bill Gilbride, a partner at Abbott Nicholson, is one of those leaders pushing back. Bill said, "It's assumed that someone who is accomplished in law school is ready and able to manage his or her time effectively. That's not necessarily the case. You need to be present and accountable as a young lawyer. Try to beat your boss to work by one minute and let your boss leave first. You need to establish your credibility by putting in face time, then after you get established, you can start working remotely from a coffee shop."

There may come a time in the not too distant future when remote work becomes standard operating procedure. But we're not there yet. We're in a transition period, and remote working is not a working model that leaders within your firm experienced themselves as associates. Accordingly, you need to play the hand you've been dealt, and this means that you need to be conscious of the expectations of your superiors. Many of them expect you to put in significant face time.

There are good reasons for this. Being present allows you to integrate and learn the ins and outs of the firm. Understanding the history of the firm is important. Every firm has stories and lore that hold clues regarding what its members value today. I assure you that there are stories about blunders made by other associates that led to an abrupt exit from the firm. Learn from these stories and let them guide your behavior. Talking to a broad cross-section of people in your firm will also help you to understand what is required to stay on the partnership track, which is often a murky issue devoid of any clear guidelines. Being present allows you to network with colleagues in your firm and form valuable relationships as you progress in your career.

> **"The most important element of success is the consistency of your effort. You need to be all in from the start and demonstrate to others in the firm that you want to be a lawyer. You need to show a desire to integrate and get to know and work with people across offices and departments."**
> **— SCOTT WOLFSON, PARTNER AT WOLFSON BOLTON**

To integrate, look for opportunities to get involved with committees and other firm initiatives. Volunteer to interview. Show up to summer associate events and engage with the summer associates and not just other lawyers in attendance. Create the impression that you're invested in the firm's success by authentically and enthusiastically immersing yourself in the inner workings of law firm life.

Another vital aspect of firm engagement is mentorship. Erika Morabito, who is a partner at Foley & Lardner, believes that the ability of a young associate to identify and seek guidance from a mentor is essential to success. Erika emphasizes that a good mentor doesn't necessarily have to be an attorney with forty years of experience under their belt. "Align yourself with someone in the mid-level ranks," Erika suggests. "It doesn't need to be your official mentor. This is a person you trust who can provide practical tips and inside information about the people with whom you work. This person can be a great source of institutional and cultural knowledge about the firm. The natural thing is to just hang around people within your practice group and class. You need to branch out."

"Young lawyers should have a partner mentor and an associate mentor."

— BILL MCKENNA, PARTNER AT FOLEY & LARDNER

Attitude often matters as much, if not more, than competence. A lawyer who practices with enthusiasm, seeks feedback, and pitches in when needed, will be forgiven for a mistake much more quickly than one who others perceive as aloof and checked out. Be engaged, seek out the counsel of colleagues, and your efforts will be recognized.

ASK FOR HELP

While peppering your superiors with lots of questions before exhaustively running down an issue yourself is a bad idea, a big part of taking ownership is knowing when and how to ask for help. Foley & Lardner partner Daljit Doogal emphasizes the importance of seeking guidance when needed. "Young lawyers tend to be a bit shy and afraid to ask questions at times," said Daljit. "These are people who come from a background marked by high achievement and now are thrust into an environment of uncertainty. In this environment, young lawyers need to know when and how to ask for help."

While senior lawyers dislike being bothered with questions that associates could easily answer for themselves, most are happy to help when necessary. Good associates know they don't have all the answers, and successful senior lawyers were once good associates. They've been in your shoes and are willing to help under the right circumstances.

Dan Sharkey, a co-founding partner at Brooks Wilkins Sharkey & Turco, believes that learning when and how to ask questions is an essential skill for young associates. According to Dan, "One of the hardest things about being a lawyer is knowing when to ask a question and when to push ahead with the uncertainty."

Asking the right questions under the right circumstances demonstrates that you have a solid understanding of the assignment and a handle on the big picture. But don't run to the partner without first thinking through the issues yourself, and don't inconvenience the partner with frequent interruptions. Approach the partner's office as if it has a red velvet rope outside of it, not as if it's an open door. If you do have questions, get them all gathered at once, ask for a meeting time, and organize your thoughts so as not to waste the other person's time because you are scattered.

There is no award handed out to the associate who spends days running into dead ends and plunging down unproductive rabbit holes. In fact, few things irritate senior lawyers more than an associate who spins their wheels rather than seeking clarity or direction. While you want to bother the senior lawyer as little as possible, a fifteen-minute interruption is far better, for all involved, than three days of research and writing that doesn't get to the heart of the matter. By asking the right questions at the right time, you'll demonstrate that you embody the adage of "working smarter, not harder." Be judicious but ask questions when necessary.

DON'T BE AFRAID TO SAY NO

The practice of law is stressful and demanding. Sometimes you need periods to decompress and catch your breath. Don't hide in your office for too long though. If you're slow, volunteer to help out. Pitch in. Show some initiative. Take ownership.

While you shouldn't hide from new work, you also shouldn't be afraid to say no. Learning when and how to say no is critically important, and it's a skill you need to develop.

If you're too busy to take on a new client matter, or non-billable project, then say so. The implications of taking on something you can't follow through on will be exponentially worse than any impression created by saying no. (Note: This presumes you are, in fact, too busy.)

Foley & Lardner partner Bill McKenna believes that many young lawyers get themselves into trouble because they worry about not having enough work on their plates, which leads them to take on too much. Bill uses surfing as an analogy: "You can't lag behind or you'll miss every wave. But if you're too aggressive and not thoughtful, then you'll get overloaded and end up with a monster wave that you can't handle." To Bill, learning to say no in the right circumstances is an important skill for a young lawyer to learn. After all, saying yes when you should say no doesn't just impact you in isolation. If you can't handle what's on your plate, then you're neither serving your client, nor the partner with the client relationship.

Saying no can be hard, whereas it's easy to say yes. From an early age we're taught to say yes and adopt a "can-do" attitude. Ambitious young lawyers often fall into this trap. Don't try to be a hero. There will be enough times in your career that you're overloaded and have no choice but to stay up all night and outwork your obligations through sweat, caffeine, and sheer will. But to take on this sort of stress frequently and voluntarily? That's a self-inflicted wound.

Take a deep breath and think carefully before saying no. Ask a few questions. Take stock. Just because you're running around with your hair on fire at the moment doesn't mean you won't have some capacity in a couple of days once the deposition is over or the deal has closed. It would be a mistake, and a missed opportunity, to turn something down just because you blurt out a panicked "no."

Use good judgment when juggling multiple assignments for different lawyers. According to Scott Wolfson, "When there are competing deadlines, ask how to proceed. First in time should not always take priority. Communicate with your assigning lawyers. Never make these judgments on your own. Don't assume an assigning lawyer knows what else is on your plate, so let them make decisions once they have the facts."

How should you say no? Be direct, honest, and respectful. Don't embellish how busy you are. It's easy enough to verify otherwise. Don't, unless asked, describe everything else you're working on and for whom. It comes off as defensive and makes the person you're turning down feel like a lesser priority. Say no, but offer to follow up and help out once your schedule frees up.

DON'T (NECESSARILY) AVOID THAT NOTORIOUS PARTNER

There's at least one partner, sometimes many, in every law firm who has a reputation that sends associates scurrying for cover. A cross between Bill Lumbergh from *Office Space* and Miranda Priestly from *The Devil Wears Prada*. Demanding. Exacting. Difficult. When their name pops up on caller ID, it invokes a moment of terror and forces a quick decision, fraught with risk: "Should I answer or send to voicemail?"

However, reputation does not always equal reality. There's a big difference between having high expectations, on the one hand, and being rude, condescending, and unfair on the other.

Partners with high expectations for associates are usually top performers. They are busy. They have lots of business. They are often on the road. Many are involved in firm and practice group administration. It's no wonder they're brusque!

According to Foley & Lardner partner Erika Morabito, "Young lawyers need to learn to adapt to different audiences. They need to act like chameleons, and act and work in a manner appropriate to the audience." This is particularly important when working with a challenging, demanding partner.

I worked for a difficult partner. He had tons of business, shuttled from city to city, and didn't accept anything less than excellence. There were plenty of times when I resented what I considered to be his unreasonable demands. Sometimes the demands were objectively unreasonable, even by large law firm standards. But other times I was just being unreasonable myself. Fifteen years, three kids, and lots of life and work experience later, and I get it. There's no other way he could have managed things. At his level, with that many balls in the air to juggle, he had no choice. It was hard, but I ultimately earned his respect, and through this experience I came to appreciate that working for a difficult partner who pushes you to get better is often one of the best ways to climb the career ladder in a law firm. It won't be easy, but if your objective is to advance and make partner at your firm, then you'll need to hitch your cart to senior allies who wield power. Many who fit this bill are "difficult."

Dealing with difficult partners is a fact of law firm life, which is all about trade-offs. Want to make partner? There's going to be some pain and suffering along the way, often resulting from working with a difficult partner. By stepping up to the challenge, you can demonstrate that you have what it takes to persevere under difficult circumstances.

YOU HAVE NO IDEA HOW MUCH PARTNERS VALUE ASSOCIATES WHO TAKE OWNERSHIP

Hopefully, you've come to appreciate that partners prefer associates who take ownership of their work. But you may have no idea just how much partners value good associates.

Because partners are so busy, they need the support of good people below them. Partners compete for the best associate talent. They jealously guard their teams. Their success depends on it. Bottom-line: They notice. They know who you are, for good or for bad.

> **"Create a habit of understanding a partner's needs. Stay focused on their preferences. Make life easy for them. Make them look good."**
> — NAT SLAVIN, FOUNDER AND PARTNER AT
> WICKER PARK GROUP

In other words, you'll know whether others perceive you as an Essential Associate who takes ownership because you'll start to assume responsibilities that would only fall to an associate who has earned the trust of the partner who is responsible for the outcome of the matter. Conversely, an associate who ducks responsibility and does sub-par work for two years is often surprised to learn during an annual review that they weren't operating under the radar screen.

There's too much at stake, and partners are too busy, to tolerate associates who aren't getting the job done. For example, Brooks Wilkins Sharkey & Turco partner Dan Sharkey urges young lawyers to, "Never draft something and say you weren't able to 'take it very far.' Never do this on the due date. When you give a partner a draft it must be your best work. Take things to the goal line."

If a partner doesn't sleep well due to stress caused by an associate who isn't cutting it, they won't be working with that associate for long. Soon that associate will find themselves without senior allies who request their help. Instead, others will perceive them as more of a commodity whose job it is to fill in gaps rather than to add value. As Felicia Perlman explained, the impact of small mistakes and errors in judgment compound over time, eroding trust in the associate. "Associates often fail to realize that it's not just the small mistake that matters," Perlman says. "It's that once you've made the small mistake a partner won't believe that your work can be trusted, and therefore won't give you work that matters."

The flip side is that associates who gain trust and demonstrate that they are reliable gain power and autonomy. Such associates are in short supply, so partners value them greatly.

An Essential Summary and Action Steps

1. Clients are becoming increasingly resistant to paying for "on the job training" for young associates. At the same time, law firms expect associates to generate a positive return on investment. Given these circumstances, young associates must bring an intense focus to their work to be both productive and effective. One of the most important ways to do this is to demonstrate accountability by taking ownership over every aspect of your work.

2. See the big picture. Don't just complete your discrete task in a vacuum. Talk to the partner-in-charge and the client to understand the big picture objectives. This will put you in a position to not only produce outstanding work product but also impact the overall strategy of the matter.

3. Seek out leadership roles in your firm. Interview job candidates, volunteer for committees, and ask your supervising attorney to lead a particular aspect of a deal or case. Show initiative.

4. Be engaged in your work environment. Particularly early in your career, this means being present in the office so that you can demonstrate your commitment to the firm's success.

5. Run down every issue as far as you can to demonstrate ownership of your work. Then, if you do have questions, get them all gathered at once. Ask for help if you need it.

6. Don't be afraid to say no. Learning when and how to say no is critically important, and it's a skill you need to develop. The implications of taking on something you can't follow through on will be exponentially worse than any impression created by saying no. Be direct, honest, and respectful when you need to say no, and offer to follow up and help out once your schedule frees up.

7. If your objective is to advance and make partner at your firm, then you'll need to hitch your cart to senior allies who wield power. Many who fit this bill are "difficult." Don't shrink from opportunities to work with difficult partners. By stepping up to the challenge, you can show others that you have what it takes to persevere and succeed under difficult circumstances.

8. Partners are busy. They need the support of good people below them. They compete for the best associate talent. They jealously guard their teams because their success depends on it. They're not ignorant of, or ambivalent to, your performance. Always do your best.

Looking for More Evidence that Taking Ownership is Important?

Jeff Barlow, former general counsel of Fortune 500 company Swagelok, and now founder of his consultancy, Nimble Services, shares his thoughts on what it takes to become a valuable, Essential Associate from a general counsel's perspective in the following essay.

Inexperienced lawyers can bring value to an in-house law department in three ways:

1. Make life easier for the in-house lawyer

2. Have a mastery of the facts of the matter

3. Be accountable and take responsibility

I worked with many inexperienced lawyers during my time as a general counsel and also as an in-house counsel. The ones that stood out, made an impact, and received additional work were ones that made my life easier, and had a mastery of the facts at all times. They also were accountable and took responsibility for errors that may have occurred along the way.

A valuable lawyer makes life easier for those around them. This includes the client and other law firm lawyers they are working with. If you are working on a research assignment for an in-house counsel, DO NOT make them hunt and search through seventeen pages of text to find a conclusion and recommendation. In-house lawyers are often running from one meeting to the next, and out of necessity have to scroll through their phones while walking to the next meeting to find your answer. If they can't find the conclusion and recommendation with ease, they will be annoyed and aggravated. They need the conclusion and recommendation at the beginning. They've outsourced the work because they don't have the capacity to do it themselves. Don't make them work to find your conclusion and recommendation. I would think the partners at your firm would prefer this as well.

A valuable lawyer makes sure they know the client's expectations. You make our lives easier if you have a clear understanding of our expectations. If the expectations we've set are not clear to you at the outset of the assignment, please ask us to clarify. Nothing is more annoying to an in-house lawyer than to receive a deliverable from a legal service provider only to find it's not on point. This causes enormous disruption at the company. We set expectations for our business partners (our internal clients) based on what we've asked for and when we expect to receive it. If we get something back from a legal service provider that either isn't what we asked for or is unusable, it throws things off internally. We then are often questioned why we used that law firm or that lawyer. It harms our reputation and yours, even when it's caused by an innocent mistake at the outset. The impact of that minor mistake can be huge.

If you have a mastery of our facts, you stand out as well-prepared and valuable. If I have to remind you of our facts, or if I feel I know our facts better than you do over the course of our matter, I start to wonder, "Why are we paying to have you around?" Dig in, roll-up your sleeves and know our facts backward and forward. This is an immense help as we discuss strategy, arguments, negotiation positions, and potential pitfalls. As in-house counsel, we encounter a large volume of issues on a daily basis. It's hard to remember every relevant fact for each matter. This is why we're paying a legal service provider. Be our expert. If you can master our facts, you'll stand out, and we'll want you working on the next matter for us because we know we'll get high-quality service. If you don't, you'll be just another lawyer that we can't remember the name of, but we're sure we overpaid.

A valuable lawyer is accountable and takes responsibility. A valuable lawyer proofreads and double-checks EVERYTHING. Emails, memos, agreements, and pleadings MUST be proofread, double-checked, and spell checked. Do NOT blame someone else if you send us work product riddled with typos or sentences that don't make sense. Take responsibility for the errors. If you blame someone else, we know we can't trust you. Careless errors waste our time (because we usually have to fix them ourselves). We don't have time to send it back to you to fix, plus we don't want to have to pay for extra work. If you make a larger error or oversight, bring it to our attention as quickly as possible and HAVE A PLAN to fix it. Don't just toss us a grenade and run—or worse ask us how it should get fixed. You'll make a name for yourself but in a negative way. Mistakes happen. As in-house counsel, we see it and live with it every day. It's how you handle those mistakes that sets you apart. Coming to us with a plan on how to fix mistakes is proving your value and demonstrating that we're in this together.

3

Be Resilient

"A gem cannot be polished without friction,
nor a man without trials."

– SENECA

ne of America's most famous innovators was a failure. Thomas Edison failed all of the time—or at least that's how it appeared to the outside world. Edison created nearly 10,000 unsuccessful prototypes before finally refining a commercially viable light bulb. Of this work, Edison said, "I have not failed 10,000 times. I have not failed once. I have succeeded in proving that those 10,000 ways will not work. When I have eliminated the ways that will not work, I will find the way that will work."

This kind of mindset is necessary to tackle any challenging endeavor, including the practice of law. You can't succeed as a young lawyer if you're not resilient because this profession is full of pitfalls like murky case law, difficult adversaries, picky partners, and hard deadlines. You will make mistakes and experience failure, so you need to learn how to deal with it. Being resilient means not giving up, bouncing back, and being energized by what you learned. It involves leaning into problems not shrinking away from them.

Many young lawyers are unaccustomed to, and uncomfortable with, the idea of embracing failure as a catalyst for growth. They achieved in academic environments that only reward success. They've trained themselves to become perfectionists who detest the idea of failing. As a result, they shy away from risk and tend to stay in their comfort zones. One of the significant differences between the lawyer mindset and the entrepreneurial mindset is that successful entrepreneurs understand that they need to fail their way forward, while lawyers avoid failure at all cost.

To grow is to fail and to fail is to grow. You can't have one without the other. As Oprah once said, "Failure is another stepping stone to success."

This is not to say that you should aspire to failure. The consequences of your actions as a lawyer are far too great to have a cavalier attitude about your work. Just understand that if you are growing, stretching, and expanding your capabilities by taking on an ever-increasing level of responsibility, you will fail from time to time. There is no way around this. Be resilient in the wake of failure and don't allow fear to stop you from acting in the first place.

Resilience is one of the essential attributes of almost all successful people. Entrepreneur Sara Blakely is an example of someone who exhibits tremendous resilience. She's the founder and still one hundred percent owner of billion-dollar brand Spanx. She knew nothing about the women's fashion and accessories market when she got started.

By the time she developed her signature women's undergarment product, she had been selling fax machines door-to-door for seven years. Selling fax machines to small businesses was, as you might expect, an undertaking that involved long bouts of failure interspersed with fleeting moments of success. Lots of resilience was required.

To get started with her new venture, she created a rough prototype by cutting the feet off a pair of pantyhose but needed to find a manufacturer who could help her produce a polished product. She did an Internet search for "hosiery mills" in North Carolina and started cold-calling with no success.

Eventually, she took a week off from her sales job and drove from mill to mill in North Carolina, figuring that she would have more luck if she could get her product idea in front of the right person at a manufacturer. Again, she was rejected. It was only after one of the mill owners, who turned Blakely down after meeting her in person, discussed the idea with his teenage daughters—who immediately recognized its brilliance—that she found someone willing to help.

When it came time to sell her new undergarment, she once again fell back on what she knew, and picked up the phone and cold-called a buyer from Neiman Marcus. It took her a week to get through, but when Blakely got the buyer on the phone, she talked her way into a ten-minute product pitch in Dallas. Her dogged persistence paid off as Neiman Marcus agreed to sell Spanx in seven stores. This was Blakely's first sale and her billion-dollar juggernaut was born.

Blakely is the epitome of resilience. She experienced lots of setbacks and ran up against brick walls, but found ways over, around, and through them. For example, at the same time that Blakely was trying to manufacture her product, she was attempting to patent it as well, but couldn't find a patent lawyer in Georgia who would take her on as a client at a price she could afford. She took matters into her own hands and bought a book about patents, did most of the patent application work herself, and went back to one of the lawyers she previously met and got the original Spanx patent filed for $700.

Blakely attributes her resilience to her father, who sat her down at the dining room table every week and asked her the following question: "What did you fail at this week?" He didn't focus on her successes. He celebrated her failures. He wanted to know that she was trying new things, stretching her capabilities, and not stuck in her comfort zone.

Coincidentally, Blakely's dad is a lawyer, and she aspired to be one as well, but she scored so poorly on the LSAT (twice), that she ditched the idea. She failed at the LSAT, but instead of wallowing she set off on a path that led to a billion-dollar opportunity.

Resilience is what allows lawyers to manage stress, battle through tough times, bounce back from adversity, and achieve success despite difficult circumstances. But what if you don't consider yourself to be a resilient person? I have good news for you—resilience is something you can develop.

Recent research into resilience has found that it is not an innate characteristic, but rather something that you can nurture. Dr. Steven Southwick, a professor of psychiatry at Yale School of Medicine, and Dr. Dennis Charney, dean of the Icahn School of Medicine at Mount Sinai Hospital, have studied resilience for more than twenty years. From POWs to special forces operators, they've examined why and how some people crumble in the face of tough situations and others emerge unscathed, and often better, from the experience. They detailed their findings in a book called *Resilience: The Science of Mastering Life's Greatest Challenges*.

Southwick and Charney found that resilient people tend to be optimistic. But it's not naive, rose-colored glasses optimism. It's the ability to have a positive outlook while still maintaining a real-world outlook. Southwick and Charney dub those with this ability "realistic optimists." Realistic optimists are those who know when to cut their losses and focus on solving problems that are within their control.

As a young lawyer, you'll face considerable adversity. The practice of law is an adversarial endeavor. It involves dealing with clients who are grappling with problems or high stakes opportunities, and sparring with other lawyers whose job it is to identify and exploit your mistakes. Even if you do everything right, you still may lose. That's the nature of the practice. You need to be able to confront challenges with a realistic optimism that enables you to focus on the problems you can solve, and not dwell on the past and fixate on things you can't control.

One of the risks young lawyers face is descending into a defensive posture brought on by doubt and despair. To grow and thrive as a lawyer, you need to remain confident about your abilities, even—no, *especially*—in the face of adversity.

OVERCOMING IMPOSTOR SYNDROME

Athletes often remark that each time they advance to the next level of competition the game speeds up. The leap from high school to college ball is a significant one. Players are bigger, faster, stronger, and the game moves at a more rapid pace. College to pro is even more drastic, as things move at a dizzying speed.

You've just turned pro. The competitive academic playing field is nothing compared to the competitive professional one you're now playing on. At times you'll feel like you don't belong. You'll soon hear, if you haven't already, a voice in your head that tells you that you're not good enough. It typically creeps in as soon as you step out of your comfort zone, and whispers warnings that you don't belong, that you don't deserve it, and that you're a fraud.

The voice cuts you down while building others up. It tells you that those around you are smarter, better, and more talented than you are, and that they have it all figured out. If you listen to the voice, you end up staying safely within your comfort zone and never move forward.

Psychologists Pauline Clance and Suzanne Imes call this type of fear "the impostor syndrome." They describe it as a feeling of "phoniness" in people who perceive themselves as not intelligent, capable, or creative, despite evidence of high achievement. People who feel like impostors live in fear of being exposed as frauds.

If you've ever stepped in front of a podium to address an audience, or taken on a job that you're not sure you can handle, then you've likely felt like an impostor. After I wrote my first book, I had to push back doubts about why anyone would be interested in reading what I had to say. This feeling of inadequacy or incompetence doesn't just affect people in a professional setting. Virtually every first-time parent wonders why their doctor allows them to bring their child home without proper adult supervision.

The most important step in overcoming impostor syndrome is realizing that we are all impostors. No one knows what they are doing most of the time. For people who routinely step out of their comfort zones, uncertainty is a constant.

Peer down the halls of your office. Look into the eyes of your colleagues. Talk to people. Almost everyone feels like an impostor to some extent. As screenwriter William Goldman once said, "Nobody knows anything."

If you can come to grips with the fact that those around you are feeling the same sense of anxiety and insecurity that you are, then pushing through the uncertainty becomes easier. Instead of succumbing to self-doubt, embrace it. There's no other way to exhibit resilience as a lawyer. Successful people of all types "fake it 'til they make it," so just keeping moving forward.

BE STOIC ABOUT IT ALL

For many young associates, their first "real" job is at a law firm. If you fall into this group, it's likely that you're receiving honest (sometimes glowing, sometimes harsh) feedback about your work for the first time. On the other hand, you may be receiving no feedback at all. It's up to you to discern the meaning of the direct, indirect, or complete lack of feedback about your performance. This means you need to understand the personality, quirks, and traits of the person delivering it (or not delivering it, as the case may be).

When I was a young associate, every time I sent an email containing work product to a partner or client, I would eagerly anticipate a "pat on the back" email arriving in my inbox. You're probably not surprised to learn that such emails rarely appeared.

That's life in a law firm! But it's a lesson that took me time to learn. Too often, I found my mood shifting with the wind—and whims—of the day's feedback. What I eventually learned is that as a law firm associate you need to learn to look for approval within yourself, and not from external sources. In other words, you need to learn to be a stoic associate.

Stoicism is a 2,000-year-old philosophy pioneered by the Greeks and popularized by the Romans. Stick with me here—Stoicism is not the stuff you learned in Philosophy 101 from a professor in a tweed jacket. It's a philosophy for the real world, and it's having a rebirth as a tool that's helping people, from NFL coaches to technology entrepreneurs, master their emotions and make the best use of their time. You've probably seen the following quote in a business article or laid over an inspirational photo on social media: "Luck is what happens when preparation meets opportunity." It comes from Seneca the Younger, a well-known Stoic thinker.

At the root of Stoicism is the practical idea that we should work to distinguish between the things that are within our control and those that are not, and to focus only on the former. Put another way, we can't always control circumstances, but we can control how we respond to them.

Whatever you do, don't get too high or too low from feedback, and don't reflexively get defensive and offer up excuses when receiving criticism. Despite the idiosyncrasies of individual lawyers, most law firms operate as meritocracies. If you fall down, you must own up to your shortcomings, failures, and disappointments, and even suck it up from time to time when you don't do anything wrong but get blamed anyway. In most instances, the excuses will outweigh, compound, or at a minimum draw more attention to the problem that you were dealing with in the first place.

The last thing you want is to get tagged as an associate who doesn't own up to their responsibilities, doesn't accept criticism well, or tries to pass the buck. Recall former Swagelok general counsel Jeff Barlow's advice to own up to mistakes and figure out a solution. The consequences of trying to pass the buck are almost always worse than those that result from making an honest mistake or two while grinding away in a stressful profession.

Don't be disappointed by lack of feedback in the wake of a job well done. If you're kicking butt, people will notice. Be stoic about it, and keep doing what you're doing.

Epictetus was one of the most interesting and influential Stoic philosophers. Despite being born a slave, he had a major influence on the thinking of another famous Stoic, Roman emperor Marcus Aurelius, who was far above Epictetus' station in life.

Epictetus faced many challenges but never got too high or too low. He understood what he could control and what he could not, and expressed this understanding as follows: "Some things are in our control and others not. Things in our control are opinion, pursuit, desire, aversion, and, in a word, whatever are our own actions."

If your happiness, your job satisfaction, and your ability to bounce back from adversity are based on a need for outside affirmation, then you're putting your success in the hands of others, instead of assuming ownership yourself.

BOUNCING BACK FROM YOUR FIRST ENCOUNTER WITH A BULLY LAWYER

Almost every young lawyer will have an encounter with a "bully lawyer," so it's important to prepare for it. Dealing with difficult adversaries is one of the greatest tests of a young lawyer's ability to remain resilient.

My first experience dealing with a bully lawyer, which I define as a lawyer who is "unreasonably difficult to deal with and attempts to exploit the fact that they are dealing with a lawyer who is far less experienced," occurred a few weeks into my career. Things were crazy. Not only was I crushed with work, but I was also still trying to find my way around the office, let alone the Bankruptcy Code. My head was spinning. Nonetheless, I started getting into the swing of things after a couple of weeks. Or so I thought.

One of my first projects involved drafting a relatively routine bankruptcy motion to reject an executory contract for a corporate debtor. A few days after filing and serving the motion, I received a call from counsel to the counter-party to the contract. He immediately lit into me, accusing me of filing a frivolous pleading, threatening sanctions, and questioning my qualifications.

This shook me up. This guy was no rookie. At the end of our conversation, I was sure that I had messed up, and that my legal career was going to be short-lived.

After gathering myself, I put the incident into perspective and saw it for what it was, which was an attempt to gain an advantage by scaring the crap out of a new lawyer. After talking to one of the partners on the case, I settled down, and things ended up fine. The court granted our motion.

If you are a junior lawyer, there are a few things you can do to prepare for your first encounter with a bully.

1. Accept that it will happen—it's inevitable. When, not if, you deal with a bully, maintain your composure and professionalism, and don't take the bait. If it's a litigation-related matter, accept that the dispute may end up before the court, so prepare yourself with the facts and the law. Don't do or say something rash that makes its way into the court record. Distinguish yourself as the clear-eyed, reasonable, and composed advocate.

2. Be professional but not a pushover. Don't shrink from the encounter and be intimidated. It's okay to punch back, as long as it's done professionally. Just like in the schoolyard, if you stand your ground your bully-adversary may shrink away, realizing that their tactics won't work on you.

3. Seek advice. Everyone has been through it, so talk to an experienced lawyer in your firm. You may be convinced after speaking to the bully—like I was—that you screwed up. But the odds are that you didn't. And even if you did, it's better to deal with it right away. Most mistakes are resolvable if caught early.

Around six months after my 2001 incident, I felt like I was hitting my stride; no bully lawyer was going to push me around again. That's when I encountered someone with a more nuanced approach. (Note: what follows is a bit more detail about the situation that gave rise to my "15 minutes of fame" referenced in the Introduction).

After six months on the job, most young associates get their "sea legs" and start to feel a bit more comfortable. Hopefully, this has been your experience (or will be). They start to learn how things work, have generated a fair amount of work product, have worked their way through a few challenges, and begin getting more individual responsibility. In my case, I was inheriting roles from more senior lawyers who were transitioning from the case I was working on to other matters.

One of the roles involved resolving claim objections (hundreds of them) in a Chapter 11 bankruptcy case, which required lots of phone conversations and correspondence with opposing counsel. One call was from a partner at a large law firm in my hometown of Detroit who called to inquire about the status of his client's claim, and our claims reconciliation process. Trying to be helpful and courteous to a fellow Michigander, I explained the claims process and promised to look into his client's claim and get back to him.

I received another call from him a couple of days later. I thought it was a bit odd that he called back so quickly. Things were busy, and I hadn't looked into the status of this particular claim. I apologized for not responding sooner and promised to be in touch later that day. When I looked up the claim, I learned that we had objected to it, and it had been disallowed two months earlier.

I called back and broke the news to the guy. His client's claim was disallowed and therefore not entitled to a recovery in the bankruptcy proceeding. He started asking me a litany of questions: "Why didn't I get served with the claim objection? Why didn't you tell me this in our initial conversation? What should I do now? Is there any way to fix this?"

I answered his questions as best I could and tried to be helpful. I explained that, if he was so inclined, he could file a motion with the Bankruptcy Court asking for relief.

Based on our records, he was served with a copy of the objection, but I didn't see any harm in letting him know that other creditors had sought relief under similar circumstances. It never really occurred to me why I needed to explain this to a bankruptcy lawyer with twenty-five years more experience than me—perhaps you see where this is going.

Two weeks later he filed a motion. The motion and accompanying affidavit were filled with my name and summaries of our conversations, as well as email correspondence between us. The motion asserted that he had never received a copy of the objection, and not-so-subtly implied that I had consented to the relief his client was seeking.

This was a big wake-up call. I was naive and didn't see our correspondence for what it was, which was the groundwork for him to try to wriggle out of a jam. It's tough to claim a conspiracy to your superiors and your client without coming across as weak, so I just had to take the heat and move on. The situation got resolved, but I learned a valuable lesson along the way, which is to never let your guard down. When backed into a corner, adversaries can do desperate things. Some will go to great lengths to try to make their problems yours.

Most of the lawyers you'll deal with on the other side will be great. They'll try to gain whatever advantage they can over you, but will do so in an honest, courteous, and respectful manner, knowing that it's generally futile to act unprofessionally.

Some adversaries will try to take advantage of you. Be aware, but don't be jaded. It happens to everyone.

> "When dealing with a difficult adversary, never make it personal. Don't take the bait and engage. Rise above it. Acting like a professional is the best revenge of all."
>
> — SCOTT WOLFSON, PARTNER AT WOLFSON BOLTON

So what should a young lawyer take away from this situation?

Be extremely careful in your conversations and correspondence. Assume every word you speak and write will find its way into the court record. Protect your client, and yourself, at all times. Again, be courteous, but leave it up to your adversary to figure out the manner in which they should proceed. Take it from me—it's no fun to see your name in a pleading filed by an adverse party unless it's part of the proof of service.

Most of all, be resilient. When something like this happens, it's not the end of the world. Your colleagues will rally around you and will help you navigate out of the morass. The key is to learn and grow from the situation, and not lose confidence.

An Essential Summary and Action Steps

1. As a young lawyer, you'll face considerable adversity. The practice of law is, by definition, an adversarial endeavor. It involves dealing with clients who have problems or high stakes opportunities and sparring with other lawyers whose job it is to identify and exploit your mistakes. Even if you do everything right, you still may lose. That's the nature of the practice. You have to confront challenges

with a realistic optimism that enables you to focus on the problems you can solve, and not dwell on the past and fixate on things you can't control. Be resilient.

2. There will be times when you feel like you have no idea what you're doing. You'll suffer from "impostor syndrome." It helps to know that all lawyers feel this way from time to time. If you can come to grips with the fact that those around you are feeling the same sense of anxiety that you are, then pushing through the uncertainty becomes easier. Instead of succumbing to self-doubt, embrace it. Keep moving forward.

3. You'll be dealing with lots of tough circumstances as a young lawyer. Work to distinguish between the things that are within your control and those that are not, and focus only on the former. Be stoic. You can't always control your circumstances, but you can control how you respond to them.

4. Most of the lawyers you will encounter will be great—zealous advocates for their clients, but courteous and professional in the process. Unfortunately, this will not always be the case. In all of your actions, interactions, and correspondence, be careful and protect your client, your firm, and yourself.

4

Be Productive

"Lost time is never found again."

– BENJAMIN FRANKLIN

During my first year of law school, my real property law professor gave a lecture in which he remarked on Judge Richard Posner. Posner is a longtime (and at times controversial) Seventh Circuit judge, author, academic, and intellectual. During the lecture, my professor discussed how prolifically Posner writes books and articles while balancing the demands of teaching and serving as a sitting judge.

Posner hasn't slowed down in the twenty years since that property law lecture. Over the course of his career, he has written more than fifty books, over 500 articles, and close to 3,000 majority opinions.

Regardless of what you think of the merits of his arguments, it's impossible not to marvel at Posner's rigor and disciplined approach to his work. Many have remarked on Posner's productivity, but few have explained how he does what he does. How does Posner balance the demands of writing, teaching, and serving as a judge while producing not just busywork, but copious amounts of work of great depth? I believe the answer lies in a profile of Posner written by Lincoln Caplan for *Harvard Magazine*, which describes Posner as someone who minimizes distractions as much as possible so that he can devote undivided attention to his most important priorities. Focused intensity free of distraction is the only way someone can produce work at such high levels of quantity and quality.

The type of deep work that Posner prioritizes (as opposed to paper-pushing busywork and email whack-a-mole) is the type of work that young lawyers must also focus on. Deep work is increasingly valuable in today's knowledge economy. For law firms to justify their high fees, they can't just provide information to a client; they need to impart wisdom and devise strategies that further the client's business objectives.

Information is plentiful. Wisdom is scarce. Accordingly, wisdom is valuable and commands a premium.

There was a time not long ago when things were different, and lawyers and law firms had a bit more wiggle room. It was a time when hourly rates increased year after year, junior associates could bill time without question, and it was considered unprofessional to try to poach another firm's clients. Times have changed.

While many lawyers lament these circumstances and see a glass half empty, others see them for what they are: a massive opportunity.

Lawyers, both young and old, who distinguish themselves by consistently producing valuable work, as opposed to busywork, will increasingly stand out to colleagues and clients. To generate valuable work, a lawyer must, like Posner, minimize distractions to devote full attention to their most important priorities. A lawyer must be highly productive to be highly effective.

MINIMIZE DISTRACTIONS

J.J. Watt is a defensive end for the NFL's Houston Texans. He is one of the league's top players and is widely regarded as one of greatest defensive players of all time. Watt's 2014 season was particularly noteworthy. Despite frequently being double-teamed by opponents, he racked up more than twenty quarterback sacks, which ranks in the top ten in the league for most sacks in a season. He even scored five touchdowns in 2014, which is a level of production that would please many running backs and wide receivers. Watt had even more to celebrate in 2014 beyond his remarkable on-field success. At the beginning of the season, Watt signed a $100 million contract extension with the Texans, which at the time was a record deal for a defensive player.

You might expect that an athlete coming off a monster season during which he signed a huge contract would spend at least a bit of time celebrating his success during the off-season. What did Watt do with his newfound riches? He bought a minimalistic rustic cabin in what he describes as "the middle of nowhere" in northern Wisconsin to double down on his work ethic, free of distraction.

While Watt is a talented force of nature, he didn't accomplish great success through talent alone. He's also one of the league's hardest working players. By putting himself in an environment that minimizes distractions, Watt can put in the hard work necessary to stay at the top of his game.

It's not just athletes who use this approach. Top performers in the knowledge economy do as well. When he was CEO of Microsoft, Bill Gates would disconnect twice a year for off-site "think weeks" during which he would do nothing but read and think deeply. Family, friends, and colleagues were not welcome. He read insights and information prepared by Microsoft associates on topics related to the future of technology and emerging product trends. Gates typically read one hundred or more papers during a think week. These sessions led to many Microsoft innovations and new initiatives.

Throughout history, deep thinkers have disconnected to minimize distractions and produce valuable work. In 1845, Henry David Thoreau headed to the woods for two years to write *Walden*. George Orwell fled the hustle and bustle of London and escaped to a remote house on the small island of Jura off the coast of Scotland to write *1984*. He described his writing sanctuary as "extremely un-get-at-able." Leonardo da Vinci spent a great deal of time wandering in nature to better understand and appreciate the world around him and train his mind to solve difficult problems. He wrote of his experience, "I roamed the countryside searching for answers to things I did not understand."

As a young, busy lawyer, I'm not suggesting that you can or should head off to a remote location in order live and work monastically. That's obviously unrealistic and inconsistent with the idea discussed in Chapter 2 that it's important to immerse yourself and be engaged within your firm's physical work environment. But to consistently produce valuable work, you need to find ways to minimize distractions.

Distractions at the office come in many forms. Relentless email. Mind numbing, soul-sucking meetings. Chatty colleagues. Facebook. LinkedIn. Phone calls. The window washing guys outside your thirty-fifth floor office who scare the crap out of you once a month (or was that just me?).

Ever go on the Internet to check out "one quick thing" and emerge from a daze twenty minutes later wondering what the hell just happened? You get the idea. In fact, that "minute or two" you intend to spend online checking Facebook is costing you much more.

According to a study conducted by Gloria Mark, who studies digital distraction at the University of California, Irvine, it takes an average of twenty-three minutes and fifteen seconds to return to your original task after an interruption. That thirty seconds spent chatting with your colleague who popped in your office? It just cost you twenty-five minutes of productivity.

Distractions have real implications. If you're frequently getting distracted, you probably end up working in fifteen-minute increments (if you're lucky) throughout the day, get little accomplished, and you're forced to begin your real work after 6 p.m. Not only do distractions crush productivity, but they can impact us emotionally as well by raising our stress levels and affecting our moods.

To avoid the "work, distraction, work, distraction" cycle that leads to late nights and unproductive days, you need to set firm boundaries—for yourself and others. Remember that every moment you spend checking social media, chatting around the water cooler, or endlessly refreshing your email inbox is robbing you of your potential to be great.

Find a Quiet Place to Work

One of the most overlooked aspects of productivity is the fact that where you work has a significant impact on how you work. If your physical environment doesn't empower and enable your goals, you'll have a hard time achieving them. Look around your office—is it built for productivity or full of distractions? Is your desk (and desktop on your computer) messy or orderly? Is your smartphone sitting on your desk, screen up and sound on, so that every notification pulls you away from your work? Is your chair positioned toward the door, so that every time someone walks by your attention gets redirected?

You can't escape the hectic law firm office environment entirely, but there are things you can do to lessen its impact on your productivity. By making a few simple changes, you can dramatically limit the number of distractions that hamper your ability to focus.

Turn Off Notifications and Use Social Media Sparingly

Social media can serve some important business purposes, such as content sharing, personal branding, and network building. It's also a fun distraction. The problem is that too many people use social media during work hours as a form of escapism that hampers productivity. Every time your phone chimes or beeps, it's a distraction. Even worse is when those notifications lead you down the rabbit hole of other people's status updates. You don't need to quit social media, just use it sparingly. Every moment spent on social networks during working hours should be purposeful and intentional. (More on this issue in chapters to come.)

Start Your Day with a Bang

The early days of my legal career involved lots of late nights at the office. It seemed like I was routinely getting home around 11 p.m., and often later. It was a busy time, so late nights were required. But not always. I slipped into a bad routine instead of crafting a good one. Looking back, staying late all of the time could have been avoided. My schedule resulted from my failure to make the necessary choices that could have helped me avoid exhaustion and burnout.

Staying late at the office creates a vicious cycle: you stay late, you get to bed late, then you get to the office late the next morning, at a time when the emails and phone calls start pouring in. You never give yourself a chance to get ahead, get organized, and get important work done when you should. Instead, you do it when you can—typically at the end of the day when things quiet down and the inputs that bombard busy lawyers stop (or at least slow down).

However, the end of the day is often the worst time to do the type of deep work that's required to get ahead in your career. Rather than doing what's most important, your day is spent doing what's most urgent. A workday spent in this fashion is like playing tennis—it feels like all you do is return volleys only to have them fired right back at you.

For most people, early morning is the best time of the day to get deep work done. You may not consider yourself a morning person, and the idea of getting to the office before 8 a.m. may sound like a nightmare, but have you considered the possibility that the reason the morning is such a drag is that you're exhausted from all of the late nights?

You can't burn both ends of the candle. It's unsustainable. You need to make a choice: Do you want a life, or do you want to spend your life at the office?

The fact that it's better to do meaningful work early in the day is a no-brainer. Literally. If you've been working all day in a stressful profession such as the law, by evening your brain is fried, your productivity sagging, and you almost certainly won't be doing your best work. Discipline is not an infinite resource. It depletes throughout the day. If you're running a long race every day that requires discipline, caffeine, or some other form of motivation to keep going at the same fast pace, then you'll always be falling behind as the day drags on like an overly aggressive marathoner who "bonks" at mile fourteen.

Don't save your most important work for the end of the day, whether it's writing a brief, practicing a presentation, or strategizing a transaction. Do it first thing, when your mind and body are fresh, then get up, take a walk, and have something to eat.

Reserve your afternoons for meetings, phone calls, and email correspondence. The perfect way to wrap up the day, hopefully by 6 or 7 p.m., is by spending fifteen minutes planning the next morning's to-do list. That way you can head home with a clear head and your next day already mapped out. The alternative is to be scattered and harried, bouncing between urgent but not necessarily essential tasks. Mediocrity is a byproduct of a distracted mind.

Your success in minimizing or eliminating as many distractions as possible is not an end in itself. You need to leverage your ability to be more productive to become more effective as an associate. You need to devote full attention to your most important priorities.

DEVOTE FULL ATTENTION TO YOUR MOST IMPORTANT PRIORITIES

Legendary UCLA basketball coach John Wooden once said, "You never want to confuse activity with accomplishment." This is solid advice to follow, but it's hard not to get caught up in the law firm activity hamster wheel.

My head used to spin as a young associate. My days would almost always start by responding to a flurry of emails that hit my inbox while I slept. I would crank out responses, grab a cup of coffee down the hall, and by the time I got back to my desk, there would always be additional emails coming in—many from people I had just responded to.

The email cycle continued throughout the day, interrupted by phone calls, meetings, timekeeping, and banter with colleagues. Before I knew it, 6 p.m. would roll around, and I had not even started the brief, presentation, or memo due the next day. Staying late all the time could have been avoided if I had not spent my days being busy. I should have been focused on my deep work priorities.

Deep Work

You've likely noticed my use of the term "deep work" a number of times in this chapter. It's not a term I came up with, but it's one that effectively describes the type of work that young lawyers who hope to distinguish themselves in a law firm must prioritize. It's a term that was popularized by author Cal Newport in his book *Deep Work: Rules for Success in a Distracted World*. Newport argues that knowledge workers, such as lawyers, who wish to succeed in the new economy must systematically move away from shallow busywork and hone their ability to "go deep" by doing challenging, substantive work.

Newport explains that two core abilities are required to excel in the new economy; namely, the ability to "quickly master hard things," and "produce at an elite level, in terms of both quality and speed."

Notice Newport's emphasis on the importance of "speed" when it comes to someone's ability to succeed and produce deep work. You can't be slow and plodding as a lawyer. You must be fast and resourceful. To become an Essential Associate, you need to be productive. It's one thing to be a young lawyer who can produce a compelling legal brief in a week; it's another to be able to do so in a day. Between the two alternatives, take a guess who partners perceive as more valuable?

The more time you can spend intensely and singularly focused on the most important work on your plate, the more valuable work you'll produce. Many lawyers spend their days doing the exact opposite, focusing on low-value, busywork tasks such as volleying email back and forth. This results in the prioritization of the urgent over the important. These types of activities feel productive, but don't produce anything of value. Busyness is not the same as productivity.

Many lawyers pride themselves on their ability to multitask. Multitasking, which is the ability to work on two or more things at once, is often heralded as a high mark of productivity. But modern research proves otherwise. In fact, we're multitasking ourselves into insignificance. Clifford Nass, a Stanford sociologist who was one of the first academics to study the effects of multitasking, conducted a study in 2009 through which he found that those who frequently engage in multitasking underperform on every measure relative to infrequent multitaskers. Nass argues that those who can't stop themselves from trying to do more than one thing at once are "suckers for irrelevancy."

Sophie Leroy, a business school professor at the University of Minnesota, also conducted a study on multitasking and found that people are less productive when they switch from one task to another instead of focusing on one thing at a time. It's pretty easy to understand why it's not a good idea to work on an important brief or deal document while at the same time participating in a conference call. You may be surprised to learn that jumping back and forth between a brief and conference calls throughout the day—no matter how much focus is applied to each task independently—also undermines results. Leroy's work proves that, even if you work on one task at a time, if you frequently toggle between tasks you'll hamper your productivity.

Our minds are not computers. We can't seamlessly transition from one task to another without carryover effects. When we switch from writing a brief, to participating on a conference call, and then back to writing the brief, we're carrying mental baggage with us from the previous task as we attempt to move forward to the new one. Leroy calls this baggage "attention residue."

A better and more productive approach is to work on one task until it is complete before switching to another. This is not always possible in a busy law firm environment. But eliminating even a bit of distraction and task-switching from your day can pay big productivity dividends.

The sum and substance of the academic research is that it's difficult, if not impossible, to engage in the type of deep work required to produce valuable work product if you're regularly switching gears—or worse, trying to drive in two gears at once. Whenever possible, focus exclusively on the task at hand.

Essentialism of Productivity

Most people try to multitask because they equate productivity only with speed without regard to the quality of output. The highest form of productivity results from a focus on both quantitative and qualitative measures. This is why productivity is not an issue of time management alone; at least it's not the lead domino.

There's never enough time in the day, and you probably can't work any harder, so it's critical to work smarter. No matter how skilled you are at managing your time, you can't manage your way through a chaotic day in a law firm without understanding the hierarchy of your priorities. In this sense, productive lawyers—*effective lawyers*—practice time curation as opposed to time management. They discern. They pick and choose. They don't multitask, they prioritize. And they ruthlessly honor, defend, and work in accordance with their most essential priorities. They do less and do it better, and because what they do is most important, they make a more significant impact.

For example, if you're working on time-sensitive legal research, it's far better to close every loop on the most important issues—*the essential ones*—in a ten page memo, than to go on for thirty pages addressing the important issues plus a whole range of extraneous ones, but all on a cursory basis. When you're hustling to meet a deadline you don't have the luxury of going down every rabbit hole. It's better to go deep on the essential few issues than wide on every issue irrespective of its importance.

David Jaffe, former general counsel at Guardian Industries, and now principal at Jaffe Counsel, believes firmly in the importance of prioritization. While thoroughness is critical, David thinks that associates who stand out to clients are those who can succinctly summarize the legal research, and then quickly transition to analyzing and contextualizing the implications of what it means in light of the particular business challenges at issue. Here's David's advice: "Condense legal issues down to a paragraph or two. Get right to the heart of the matter. Bottom-line: work effectively. It's hard for many young lawyers to realize that legal answers are not valuable any longer. What is valuable? Good judgment and specific solutions to problems."

Prioritization of tasks is what allows you to quickly get to the point. To prioritize your tasks effectively you need to have a handle on what those tasks are. That's why it's critical every morning (or the evening prior) to review what's on your plate and create a game plan for your day. You must also have a big picture view of things, which is an understanding that only can be gained by looking ahead. While a calendar is obviously an important weapon in your arsenal, it can't be one used just for daily reminders. "Day of" is not the time to become aware of a filing deadline.

LIST-BUILDING

The best way to establish priorities is to write them down. Making and using lists is the cornerstone of an efficient productivity system. You can't expect to keep everything straight in your head, so you need to get things down on paper.

Bill Gilbride is a partner at Abbott Nicholson. He's a busy and accomplished litigator and trial lawyer. For many years he also served as managing partner of the firm, which required him to manage his busy practice, as well as the administrative details of a complex enterprise. He sorts through the complexity of his schedule by systematically identifying his priorities and capturing them on a task list that he works from on a daily basis.

Bill's productivity philosophy is to start each day with the most important task on his list, which he defines as: "What is due tomorrow." If he has a court appearance the next day, he starts with tasks that enable him to prepare for it. According to Bill, "If I don't start with what's most important, then it will be 6 p.m. before I know it, and I'll be faced with the task when I'm most fatigued." He doesn't have to spend precious mental energy throughout the day trying to figure out what to prioritize next—the work he does first thing in the morning dictates what gets onto his list. Once he establishes priorities, he can flow through his day.

Bill shared the five steps he uses to ensure that he's productive, and list-building is central to his approach.

1. Maintain an ongoing task list

2. Print out task list every morning and review

3. Prioritize tasks and most important clients

4. Break down tasks into achievable steps

5. Do most important task first

By staying organized with his lists—one to capture all of his priorities, and another to guide his daily workflow—Bill can craft and then execute a strategy for each day that allows him to be productive and effective.

Attorney and productivity expert Paul Burton, whose firm QuietSpacing conducts productivity training seminars for lawyers and law firms, also shared his thoughts about the importance of list-building. Burton believes that one of the most important skills a young lawyer can acquire is the ability to simply and efficiently capture and distill the enormous amounts of data they encounter on a daily basis. "List making helps the lawyer's mind make sense of the crazy world they operate in," Burton said. "Lists quiet down the internal space in your mind and allow space to focus on and create productivity, rather than just activity. Lists should be simple and easy to use, not complex."

Lists should be organized in terms of priorities and not simply "to-dos." Bill Gilbride organizes his lists in a way that helps him identify and accomplish his day's most important tasks. Because many of us never learned a better way, we create laundry lists of to-dos that overwhelm us. This leads us to look for low hanging fruit on lists that can get done, rather than essential work that *should* get done.

This problem stems from a misunderstanding that to-do lists function as nothing more than external memory aids—a junk drawer for dumping all of the miscellaneous thoughts, tasks, and reminders swirling in our heads. Because we want to be productive—it feels good to be productive, after all—we tackle things that are quick and easy on the list, instead of those that are hard and important.

Instead of overcomplicating list-building, which can lead to less productivity, it's better to put the minimum amount of effort into a list system that will produce the maximum amount of results. To do this, let's follow the lead of nineteenth-century Italian economist Vilfredo Pareto, whose work has become known as "Pareto's Principle," also referred to as the "80/20 Principle."

The 80/20 Principle stands for the proposition that eighty percent of the benefits that we derive from an activity result from twenty percent of the effort we put into it. Put another way, a few inputs typically lead to an outsized amount of outputs. Pareto developed this insight after observing, year after year, which twenty percent of the pea pods in his garden produced approximately eighty percent of the peas. He then studied and applied the principle more broadly across other spectrums of economic activity.

You can observe the 80/20 Principle at work in most law firms, where a majority of revenue is generated from approximately twenty percent of clients, and approximately twenty percent of lawyers are typically responsible for bringing in the majority of work. The numbers may vary so don't get hung up on exact percentages, but the principle remains: All activities and investments do not create equal value. Some are *disproportionately* valuable.

Since much of what we do matters little, and a small amount of what we do matters greatly, we stand to benefit if we can be more discerning in how we spend our time. When applied to list-building, an 80/20 analysis dictates a simple, scaled-down approach, with a focus on activities that produce the most value (for example, time to think and write, as opposed to more time for processing email).

It's best to work from two lists, each of which serves its own purpose.

A "Macro" list identifies big objectives and responsibilities. This may include things like "Write summary judgment motion for XYZ case" and "Create a personal marketing plan." Each Macro objective or project should then have a number of bullet points associated with them, each of which may have corresponding sub-bullet points that identify the specific tasks required to accomplish the objective. Let's take a look at what a couple of items on a healthcare law associate's Macro list might look like:

Write article for outside publication
- Identify relevant trade publications
- Send letters and emails to editors
- Create an outline of topic ideas
    - Changes to Affordable Care Act

     – HIPAA and electronic medical records

Build a network of referral sources
- Research and register for industry conference
  - Book hotel and flight
- Send LinkedIn connection requests to relevant individuals
- Set up weekly lunch/coffee/drinks
  - Email Joe Smith
  - Send handwritten note to Sally Jones

Paul Burton calls the process of breaking down big projects into smaller ones "chunking." By chunking tasks, Burton explains, it allows lawyers to delegate work and then structure their days to tackle non-delegable projects.

A "Micro" list is a daily to-do list that identifies the specific sub-part tasks from the Macro list that you must complete on a particular day. Use your Micro list to make your day more manageable. Complete your Micro list each morning, or the evening prior, after referencing your Macro list to identify your most important priorities. Ideally, it should include three to five tasks that are ordered in terms of priority. Finish the most important one before moving on to the next.

TIME-BLOCKING

Is your calendar a productivity and organizational tool for you, or for someone else? Most lawyer's calendars are full of other people's priorities, such as meetings, phone calls, court appearances, and other appointments. It's also random. There is no methodology other than the existence of an open block of time to dictate when or how something should be scheduled.

A better way to use your calendar and plan your day is to utilize time-blocking. While list-building is a tool used to determine *what task to work on*, time-blocking focuses on *when to work on it*. Time-blocking, like list-building, is about setting priorities. To schedule your day efficiently, you need a handle on not just available time, but also the optimal time to tackle different priorities. Once you gain this understanding, you can then structure your time by your priorities.

As discussed previously, it's often best to block chunks of time off first thing each morning to engage in deep work that otherwise gets pushed off to the evening when the phone stops ringing and emails subside. If you conclude that morning is when you're at your best, your day should be structured to take advantage of your peak performance hours. Don't just tell yourself to do deep work in the morning, take the initiative to block time on your calendar so that other distractions won't derail you.

It may seem unrealistic to schedule big chunks of uninterrupted time each morning. This used to be my excuse, too. But one day I decided that a good plan was better than a perfect one, and from that day forward I've done the best I can to stick to a structured schedule that reflects my most important priorities. Once I started realizing the benefits of working in this manner, the excuses I clung to about the impossibility of time-blocking fell apart at the seams. My time-blocks for deep work became inviolable. Every day isn't perfect, and I often have to juggle and re-order my time-blocks, but unless I schedule time with myself on my calendar to address my most important work, I almost always find myself working on someone else's priorities.

POMODORO TECHNIQUE

Once you've set priorities, and blocked time necessary to focus on them, the next step is to get to work. We all have the same twenty-four hours in the day. The question is: How can we get the most done in the least amount of time?

The Pomodoro Technique is a productivity system developed by Francesco Cirillo, which he documented in a paper in 2006. It's a technique based on the "sprint/recover" work philosophy. Cirillo's big insight is that we can be more effective, often in far less time, if we work like sprinters, rather than marathoners. It's important to be patient and circumspect over the long-term of your career while at the same time moving fast during the day-to-day. That's where the Pomodoro Technique comes in. Its basic premise is that, when faced with any large task, you should break the work down into brief, timed intervals (called "Pomodoros"), with short periods for recovery in-between.

Here's how it works:

- Pick a task
- Set a timer for twenty-five to forty minutes
- Work intensely on the task during the interval
- If a distraction pops into your head, write it down, but immediately get back on task
- At the end of an interval, get up and take a short break (five to ten minutes)
- After four intervals, take a longer break (fifteen to thirty minutes)
- Sprint, then recover, to stay focused on the task at hand and sidestep the distractions that lead to a more scattered approach to your work

While twenty-five minutes of work may not seem like much, keep in mind that during these intervals you're supposed to be working intensely. No checking emails. No Internet surfing. No chit-chatting. No distractions. This may differ considerably from the multitasking approach you currently employ, which is why the Pomodoro Technique leads to different (i.e., better) results. By focusing intensely on the task at hand, and shutting out all else, both the quantity and quality of your production during these short intervals will be high.

Working in this manner has an added benefit. If you're like most people, your best ideas come during periods of recovery, when your mind is free to wander, and not in the midst of an intense work session. Ever come up with a great idea first thing in the morning in the shower, or right before you fall asleep in bed at night? A mind at rest, and free of distraction, is a powerful thing. By taking the time to recover, you can then apply these "free range" ideas during your next period of work.

As you're starting to implement the Pomodoro Technique into your day, keep this in mind: You're a human, prone to distraction, full of emotions and a creature of habit. The Pomodoro Technique may be appealing, but don't dive in too deeply from the start. You have to give yourself time to adapt to a new way of working. If you haven't been exercising, you wouldn't (or at least shouldn't) start back with a new routine that requires you to complete 500 burpees in thirty minutes. By the same reasoning, you shouldn't try to get started with the Pomodoro Technique by attempting to finish fifteen intervals per day.

Start slow. That's how new habits get formed.

UTILIZE MARGIN TIME

Successful entrepreneurs often discuss the importance of working *on their business*, and not just *in their business*. To grow, entrepreneurs need to focus on the big picture issues that often get pushed aside for the urgent financial and operational issues of the day.

Similarly, to grow in your legal career, you need to prioritize important, non-billable activities such as business development, marketing, and continuing education. But these activities often get overlooked to address hot client demands.

One solution is to block time for these essential activities. While it may not seem possible during the urgency of the day-to-day, by taking a big picture view you'll find that over the course of the year there is sufficient time for personal and professional development within the confines of the workday.

There is also margin time outside of these confines to engage in these activities. Margin time spent in the car, on the train, waiting in line, or walking to lunch can be utilized to learn and grow.

These days, almost every learning tool is digitized, and as long as you have a smartphone and a pair of headphones, you can consume it. Many audiobooks and podcasts provide valuable wisdom and insights on all manner of topics relevant to building a successful legal practice.

If you can find the time—at the margins—to tap into these resources, you'll add to your skill set, and also eliminate the stress you feel because you can't seem to fit these extracurricular activities into your workday.

SEVEN BOOKS AND PODCASTS FOR MARGIN TIME

One of the challenges of squeezing in learning during margin time is taking out the guesswork about what content to consume. Here's a list of seven books and seven podcasts that offer varied and valuable lessons on issues ranging from how to become more creative to how to become more focused at work.

BOOKS

1. *Good to Great* by Jim Collins

2. *The 7 Habits of Highly Effective People* by Stephen Covey

3. *The Lean Startup* by Eric Ries

4. *Daring Greatly* by Brené Brown

5. *Essentialism: The Disciplined Pursuit of Less* by Greg McKeown

6. *Deep Work: Rules for Focused Success in a Distracted World* by Cal Newport

7. *Creativity, Inc.: Overcoming the Unseen Forces That Stand in the Way of True Inspiration* by Ed Catmull

PODCASTS

1. Happier with Gretchen Rubin

2. The Tim Ferriss Show

3. Lawyerist

4. Masters of Scale with Reid Hoffman

5. Revisionist History with Malcolm Gladwell

6. Good Life Project

7. HBR IdeaCast

An Essential Summary and Action Steps

1. There's no perfect plan when it comes to increasing productivity. However, certain techniques and tactics—including prioritization, list-building, time-blocking, the Pomodoro Technique, and utilizing margin time—can serve as building blocks for squeezing more effectiveness and efficiency out of your day. The most important takeaway: No one is going to give you your time back. You need to take it back. If you don't establish priorities for yourself, you'll be working on someone else's. And if that's the case, you'll find yourself at the office until 10 p.m. way too often, with too little to show for it.

2. Lawyers work hard. There's no getting around this fact. But you can make life easier on yourself, and you'll become a better lawyer as a result, if you learn how to work smarter. Working smarter and more productively will require you to manage and ignore a bit of the noise around you. While there's no perfect plan, if your day feels out of control then there's almost certainly a better plan.

3. By habitually implementing some basic organizational and productivity best practices into your day, you will be able to capture information and keep it on your radar screen. Start small. Don't try to become ultra-productive from day one. The goal is to build new habits over time, not to overwhelm yourself by making drastic changes all at once.

4. Once you have a system in place for capturing information, you'll then be able to tackle your work in the most efficient manner possible. Not only will this improve your productivity, but it will also

improve your physical and mental wellbeing. You'll be less anxious and stressed. As a result, you'll sleep better, which will help you be more organized and productive, and so on. Unlike the vicious cycle perpetuated by staying late at the office all of the time, better productivity habits launch a virtuous cycle.

5. You'll come to learn in your career, if you haven't already, that a perpetual "nose to the grindstone" approach is harmful to productivity. Working all of the time doesn't make you a hero. It makes you sloppy. It impairs your judgment. It makes you cranky and unpleasant to be around. It certainly doesn't make you a better lawyer. Many outstanding lawyers are raging workaholics, but it's wrong to think that you have to be a workaholic to be an excellent lawyer. The truth is, over the long-term, decision-makers don't care if you're the top billing associate in your class. While the quantity of work remains important, there is more value placed on things like quality of work, ability to develop business, and sound judgment as you progress in your career. Pair these qualities with strong work ethic, and there's no doubt that you'll become an Essential Associate. If you just grind away and never grow, your hard work will be for naught.

6. During this period when clients are becoming increasingly resistant to paying for young associate time, your success will be determined by how much real value you're able to provide. Can you get the job done? Did you accomplish anything? Are you dependable? Quality, progress, and solutions are what matter most. Accordingly, don't be busy. Be productive.

7. It's foolish to think that you won't have to work late once in awhile.

But no lawyer should accept that every day in a law firm must end sitting at a conference room table filled with stacks of paper and littered with carry-out containers of half-eaten Thai food. A legal career is hard. The work is stressful. Don't make things harder on yourself by working in a way that is unhealthy, unsustainable, and unproductive. Get up a little earlier. Get your work done. Then get out of the office and into the world. You'll be a better lawyer—and person—for it.

5

Be Growth-Minded

"Whether you think you can, or you
think you can't, you're right."

– HENRY FORD

A ny discussion of what it takes to become an Essential Associate is incomplete without addressing an issue that looms large over the legal industry, which is the generally held belief that most lawyers are dissatisfied with their careers.

There has been a great deal written about the epidemic of "The Unhappy Lawyer." Surveys suggest that career dissatisfaction among lawyers, and even rates of depression, are on the rise. According to 2016 research from the American Bar Association, twenty-eight percent of lawyers experience mild or higher levels of depression, nineteen percent experience anxiety, twenty-three percent experience chronic levels of stress, and twenty-one percent struggle with problematic drinking.

Law firm associates are not immune from these issues. A 2013 survey by the website CareerBliss found that "Associate Attorney" was the unhappiest job in the United States, handily beating out runner-up "Customer Service Associate."

This problem is not exclusive to lawyers in the United States. Research conducted by the Junior Lawyers Division found that more than ninety percent of young lawyers in Great Britain frequently feel under "too much emotional or mental pressure" at work. More than one in four respondents described the stress as either "severe" or "extreme."

Many reasons have been proffered to explain the causes of this problem in the profession, including too many hours, stress, tedious work, and the adversarial nature of the law, to name a few.

I had my moments. There was a stretch of time early in my first year that my wife recalls (not fondly) as the "Sweatpant Period." If not at work, I'd be home in bed or on the couch in sweatpants, eyes glazed over. I was working too much and not getting enough sleep. I was out of it and unhappy. Fortunately, this period passed quickly with no real consequences. Others aren't so lucky.

Jonathan Fields is a successful author, speaker, podcaster, entrepreneur, and owner of a company called The Good Life Project. He's also a former practicing corporate lawyer at a big Wall Street firm. As an associate on the partnership track, he gave everything to his job.

Fields has written and spoken about this period in his life, including a particularly harrowing stretch of seventy-two hours of work that involved little sleep and lots of stress. He powered through the work, then went home and crashed. His body gave out. He went to the hospital and doctors discovered that a life-threatening, baseball-sized infection had eaten a hole in his intestines

For Fields, that was it. He left his firm and quit the practice of law. Fortunately, things have worked out for him, as he's gone on to have a thriving career outside of the law. The point is that this job will take everything from you if you let it.

The problems, including stress, anxiety, and depression, that run rampant within the associate ranks of the profession are apparent. But what to do about it? That's trickier. What is clear is that finding the solution is a dual responsibility of both law firms and law firm associates.

In recent years, firms have increasingly been urged to improve culture and create more opportunities for work-life balance, particularly for young associates. Firms need to change, the thinking goes, to adapt to the needs and desires of millennials and future generations of young lawyers to come.

However, this type of thinking presumes that young lawyers who fall within the arbitrary age range that defines millennials are part of some "lazy and entitled" (adjectives I've frequently heard used to describe this generation) monolith that expects to be treated more gently than members of previous generations. It's become conventional wisdom that young lawyers, today, are motivated by fundamentally different incentives than those who came before them.

I'm a skeptic of conventional wisdom. Given its propensity for being proven wrong, it should be considered an oxymoronic term. The same criticisms—"lazy and entitled"—were levied against Generation X lawyers who were lavishly recruited by law firms during the late 1990s tech boom. I suspect much the same was said of baby boomers as well. It's just another version of the "I trudged to and from school through a foot of snow" story used to mythologize the idea that some generations had it harder than others.

The truth is that today's young lawyers are fundamentally the same as those who came before them. They're individuals with different priorities and proclivities. Some desire to become powerful and make lots of money, while others seek a more flexible work experience.

The danger, therefore, is that instead of making things better, firms that implement changes with the good intention of making the practice of law a more pleasant (or at least palatable) experience for young lawyers may be making things worse. At a minimum they're attempting to solve the wrong problem.

There's no getting around the fact that the practice of law, particularly at the highest levels, is a hard grind. This hasn't changed, and probably never will. In fact, it's likely more true in today's competitive environment than it ever has been. By suggesting to young lawyers that they can have their cake (flexibility/balance), and eat it too (advancement/achievement), we're doing them a disservice. It's a missed opportunity to teach young lawyer what it takes to have a long, pleasant, and prosperous career.

UNDERSTANDING THE ASSOCIATE MINDSET

Most associates come to the practice of law straight from the world of academia. In that world, they learned to work hard, reach a milestone, and graduate to the next challenge. It was a well defined, lockstep experience.

Things change at a law firm, where future milestones are less clear. The next obvious one—partnership—seems vague and distant. But for many, it becomes a fixation, and the next tangible validation of their hard work.

This is a trap into which many lawyers fall. They're hyper-focused on achieving future milestones like making partner and making enough money to retire. They believe that by reaching these milestones they'll become content. In his book *Happier*, Tal Ben-Shahar calls this dynamic the "arrival fallacy." It relates to the belief, which often proves false, that when you arrive at a destination or obtain something tangible, you'll be happy.

The problem is that during the process of trying to reach these milestones, many trade-off present happiness for uncertain future happiness. Because they are unhappy in the journey, they tend to increase their spending along the way in hopes of numbing the pain. They then find themselves sprinting on a hedonic treadmill which robs them of the safety, security, and freedom down the road that they thought their present pain and suffering would afford them in retirement.

There is a big problem with suffering through the everyday grind of a legal career with an eye toward the rewards of an uncertain future: Namely, what if the end isn't different, but just more of the same?

LEARN TO LOVE THE PROCESS (DON'T FOLLOW YOUR PASSION)

Instead of fixating on the future, young lawyers need to learn to love (or at least like) the *process of practicing law*. For a person who learns to love the process, each day isn't drudgery; it's another opportunity for fulfillment. Partnership becomes a goal, but not an obsession, because there is satisfaction in the everyday.

"It's the journey, not the destination" may sound like a trite cliché, but it's true. As those who have trained for and run marathons will attest, it's not the end of the 26.2-mile race that most remember, and are most proud of, over the long-term. It's the hundreds of training miles that get logged in the months leading up to it. Those that try to run the race, but refuse to embrace the training, typically end up injured and disappointed even if they manage to cross the finish line. The satisfaction derives from the work, not the result. This principle applies even more acutely when it comes to the work we put into our careers because the stakes are so much higher.

One way to help lawyers learn to love the process of practicing law is to encourage them to look at their careers not as one long journey, but as a series of shorter ones. The first destination, or rung on the career ladder, is reached after approximately one to two years of practicing law. This is a point at which many lawyers feel like they're starting to get their feet underneath them, begin developing sound judgment, and have attained a basic level of competence. In other words, they're ready to move on to the next destination as a mid-level associate. It wasn't easy, but they look back with satisfaction and forward with confidence.

Other lawyers finish the first stage of their careers chastened and broken. They feel regret about their career choice, and detest the day-to-day of their job. They focus on a distant future in which more money will provide the cure to what ails them, or fixate on how to get out of their circumstances and into a job that they are more "passionate" about.

"Follow your passion" is advice that frequently gets bandied about but it's flawed. First, it presumes that someone has a single passion that can be pinpointed and leveraged into a career. Second, it suggests that because someone enjoys something as a hobby, then they will enjoy doing it as a job, too. Rarely is this the case. The realities of managing clients and customers, employees and payroll, and vendors and cash flow disabuse most people of the notion that following their passion into a job or a business is a path to success and contentment.

Presumably, you went to law school, took the bar exam, and became a practicing lawyer because you had some interest in the law. You may have even "followed your passion" to law school. Indeed, many lawyers decide to go to law school after reading a book or watching a movie or T.V. show that romanticizes the notion of what it means to be a lawyer. They become passionate about the idea of the practice of law; then once they start practicing law they become disheartened by the reality of it. Perhaps this resonates with you because you may not be feeling passionate about your career. Take solace in knowing that as you grow and get better, satisfaction will follow. You'll learn there is a passion tipping point that comes as you progress as a lawyer. You can't "find" passion. You must develop it over time.

Passion, be it for a hobby or a profession, can be developed over time by improving your skills. As you build competence, you'll come to appreciate and be fulfilled by your work, and the independence and rewards that come with it. For most of us, passion for our careers is not present from day one. It's cultivated and earned over time.

If you can buy into the idea of "cultivating" and "developing" passion, as opposed to "finding" or "following" it, then this mindset can arm you with the understanding that you can work toward building a passion for your job. This approach takes longer but can pay lifelong dividends. Successful lawyers manage to find passion in what they do, which allows them to do more of it—faster, better, and for longer—than their peers.

Getting good at something is the first step toward becoming passionate about it. Perhaps you weren't "meant" to become a lawyer in the purest sense, but over time your passion will grow, and you'll come to derive greater meaning from your work.

Hopefully, this makes intuitive sense to you. The odds are that at some point in your life you've taken up a hobby—be it golf, running, knitting, or baking—that was difficult at first. You had an interest, but not necessarily a passion that led you to pursue it. You weren't particularly good at the hobby at first, and chances are the activity wasn't that much fun until you became good at it. Eventually, as you honed your skill, you may have even become passionate about it.

Take playing the guitar, for example. Most people pick up a guitar with visions of riffing solos like Eddie Van Halen but quickly give up. That's because practicing guitar is painful and frustrating for several months until you've done enough work to build up calluses on your fingers and learn the basics. Once someone earns their calluses and their skills improve the guitar starts to become fun and satisfying. Resilience is built up during the painful periods of any worthy endeavor and serves as a bridge to the other side. If you want to do something that's satisfying, most times you have to do it when it's not.

This concept—the connection between hard work and meaning—is one that psychologist Mihaly Csikszentmihalyi studied in the early 1980s. Csikszentmihalyi conducted a series of studies meant to understand the psychological impact of common behaviors we engage in every day. One of the principal insights of his work was to show that depth generates meaning. According to Csikszentmihalyi, the best, most satisfying moments come when we stretch ourselves. Csikszentmihalyi popularized the term "flow state" to describe the feeling of effortlessness experienced by high achievers—from authors to athletes—operating at peak performance. But the psychological rewards of operating in a flow state don't come easily. Indeed, it's called "hard" work for a reason.

Any time you're learning a new skill, or building something worthwhile, it's hard. Enjoyment only comes after you've practiced it enough to get good at it. You can't just follow your passion and expect that to be enough. When engaging in a challenging career, mastery is almost always a precursor to passion. And if you want to gain mastery of the *practice* of law, you have to (you guessed it): practice, practice, practice. According to Clark Hill partner Joel Applebaum, "Young lawyers who succeed are the ones who roll up their sleeves and get their hands dirty."

It takes time to put in the practice necessary to gain mastery. In his book *Outliers*, Malcolm Gladwell popularized the idea of the "10,000 Hour Rule," which is Gladwell's explanation of how long it takes to become excellent at something. The 10,000 Hour Rule is a helpful framework for thinking about how long it takes to start excelling at the practice of law.

Think about it: Many young lawyers don't start to have a real sense of competence and autonomy until approximately their fifth year of practice. After five years, most lawyers have put in at least 10,000 billable hours on the job.

Foley, Baron, Metzger & Juip partner Randy Juip has a clear-eyed conversation with young lawyers to give them a sense of what the start of their careers will entail. "The first five years of your career will be tough, and you need to survive it," Juip said. "You'll come out of law school completely unprepared. After five years you'll be able to deal with it. You'll realize you can handle it. You can build on your experience. Once you have a handle on the mechanics, you can start working on the artistry of the law."

It's no coincidence that associates are most recruitable around their fifth year of practice, which is when they've gotten far enough along the learning curve that other firms perceive them as assets.

But it's not just time clocked that matters, it's what you do with that time that makes the difference. In some fields of work—data entry, for example—you can put in a certain amount of work to gain sufficient competence to perform your job duties adequately and then plateau. It may only take a few hundred hours of work to reach relative peak performance. In other words, no matter what you do, you won't be adding appreciably more value after 10,000 hours of work than you will after 1,000 hours. In cognitively demanding jobs such as the practice of law or medicine there is no growth ceiling to bump into, and no predetermined plateau to reach. The potential for increased performance and achievement is exponential. That's why practice is so crucial in the practice of law. But it's not just any type of practice that matters. You must engage in *deliberate practice*.

Gladwell's 10,000 Hour Rule derives from the work of Florida State University professor K. Anders Ericsson. Through his research and writing, Ericsson explained that experience, in and of itself, is not determinative of excellence. To become excellent you have to put in a lot of hours, but the time spent must be dedicated to the *type of work that matters*.

Ericsson uses the term "deliberate practice" to describe this type of work. Deliberate practice is purposeful, systematic, and requires focused attention. It must be conducted with the specific goal of improving performance. It's work that stretches you beyond your current abilities. If you're engaged in deliberate practice, you're deeply immersed in your work. You're not going through the motions. A young lawyer who incorporates the principles of deliberate practice into their legal career plans their work thoughtfully, works intensely on it, then seeks feedback from others on their performance.

Why does this matter? One of the primary reasons is that too few young lawyers approach their work and their careers deliberately, and with the mindset that *how they work* matters considerably in determining their success and satisfaction. Most ignore the fundamentals of strong performance. Accordingly, those who do adopt the principles of deliberate practice are at a distinct advantage.

While many of your peers are focused on putting in hours, you can rise above, and build a greater passion for what you do, by working systematically to develop the valuable skills required to optimize your performance. By recognizing the fundamentals of high achievement, you'll have a leg up on those who are just going through the motions.

For a corporate bankruptcy lawyer with a litigation focus such as myself, the ability to write clearly and convincingly is a valuable skill. Early in my career, I realized that the written work product produced by "pure" litigators in my firm was more polished and persuasive than what was typically filed in bankruptcy court. If I could bring my writing skills up to their standards I figured that I could stand out.

I sought the help of a litigation partner who is as an excellent writer. I asked him to review a few examples of my writing and provide feedback. What came back wasn't pretty. After reviewing his feedback, I realized that many of the problems with my writing were due to my tendency to work from a similar brief or motion that I found in the firm's archives. I would attempt to shoehorn my facts and arguments into a pre-existing template. This led to patchwork quilt pleadings that lacked the style and coherence of polished legal work product.

Moving forward, instead of trying to mimic the style of my litigation colleagues by using their work product as a starting point for my own, I adopted the *writing process* they used to produce excellent work. This process involved thinking through the issues, outlining arguments, finding research to fill in any gaps, and then, most importantly, editing ruthlessly and seeking feedback from others. Instead of starting from a template, I started from scratch to build something better. My writing improved through deliberate practice.

You can't keep doing things the way you always have and expect to get any better. Abbott Nicholson partner Bill Gilbride didn't develop a highly efficient productivity routine, which helped him manage the dual demands of a busy litigation practice and the role of managing partner, by accident. He studied, took a time management course, and refined his methods over time. Foley & Lardner partner John Trentacosta, who you'll meet in more detail in chapters to come, didn't write a successful book on Michigan contract law by wishing it into existence. Bill and John were thoughtful. They planned. They worked intensely. They made deliberate practice part of their daily practice. You can, and should, too.

Acquiring the skills required to become a stand-out lawyer and develop a passion for your career takes many years, so it's critical to start now. Doing so will set you on a path that yields tremendous rewards, both in terms career success and satisfaction, down the road.

DO YOU HAVE A GROWTH OR FIXED MINDSET?

The fundamental difference between young lawyers who are thriving and satisfied, and those who are dissatisfied and struggling, is not culture or environment—you'll find both types of people at every firm. The difference is mindset. One has learned to enjoy the process, embrace the challenges of the day-to-day, and put the work in to get better, while the other focuses only on the destination. One feels in control of their circumstances, while the other feels controlled by them. One concentrates on creating value through their work, while the other concentrates on what they can get out of their job. A young lawyer who is growing and thriving focuses on adopting and exhibiting the Five Characteristics of an Essential Associate.

To some, the list of Five Characteristics is heartening. You may recognize some or all of these characteristics as qualities that you already possess. To others, this list may be disheartening. They may believe they embody few, if any, of them. If you fall into the latter category, don't despair. You can develop the Five Characteristics; they're not immutably ingrained traits. But cultivating and manifesting them requires belief that growth is possible. In other words, you need to approach your professional development with a "growth mindset" and not a "fixed mindset."

The distinction between a growth mindset and a fixed mindset comes from the work of Stanford psychologist Carol Dweck, who synthesized her research in the book *Mindset: The New Psychology of Success*. In *Mindset*, Dweck dives deeply into the power of our beliefs, and explains that how we think about the possibility of change can have a significant impact on nearly every aspect of our lives.

Someone who holds a "fixed mindset" believes that their character, intelligence, and creative ability are static and immutable and that they have little control over outcomes in their life as a result. Put another way, and to contextualize this concept for our purposes, associates with fixed mindsets who do not consider themselves to be particularly productive do not believe they can become productive in the future.

A person with a "growth mindset," on the other hand, is motivated by challenges and sees failure as an opportunity. Someone with a growth mindset believes they can get better through the experience of trial and error.

Most successful people have growth mindsets. Having a growth mindset is almost a prerequisite for someone who hopes to succeed in a demanding profession in which failure and setbacks are inevitable.

Kamal Ravikant is a successful author, entrepreneur, and angel investor. On the "Unmistakable Creative" podcast, Ravikant explained what inspired him to write books. He always wanted to be a writer, and one day he walked into Barnes & Noble and picked up a copy of Ernest Hemingway's *Farewell to Arms*. This occurred shortly after Ravikant finished writing the first draft of his first novel. He read Hemingway's work and broke down in tears. *Farewell to Arms* revealed to him "what real writing was" and how far he had to go as a writer.

However, instead of remaining disheartened, this incident served as a wakeup call that inspired Ravikant to become the best writer he could be. It gave him a marker of where he needed to go. He spent a decade obsessively writing and rewriting his novel while collecting loads of rejection letters along the way. Eventually, he published the book (and many others) and became a bestselling author.

Law firm associates with fixed mindsets look at successful lawyers in their firms and are daunted and discouraged by the gap between where they perceive themselves to be in their careers and where the successful lawyers already are. Associates with growth mindsets recognize the gap between where they are and where they want to go, but rather than being discouraged by it, they're motivated to get better. They know that the qualities and characteristics—things like accountability and discipline—that made the lawyers successful can be cultivated through hard work and practice. They do not become disheartened by their shortcomings. In fact, they don't perceive them as shortcomings at all; to them, they're opportunities for learning and growth.

ARE YOU READY TO GROW?

Chances are, no one handed you a playbook that lays out what you need to know to become an excellent lawyer when you started your career (although I'm hopeful that this book will now serve as one). Many of these lessons will have to be learned the hard way, through struggles and mistakes. Growth will come slowly, which is why patience and a long-term perspective is required. You may feel discouraged because the passion you thought you had for the practice of law seems to be waning as the realities of the challenging career you've chosen are setting in.

Keith Lee, attorney at the Hamer Law Group, and author of the Associate's Mind blog, describes the trials that young lawyers face when starting their careers. "They're forced to step up and do things they're not used to or necessarily equipped for," Keith said. This challenge is particularly acute for those Keith calls "KJD" lawyers—which is an acronym for "Kindergarten to Juris Doctor"—who start their careers straight out of law school with no full-time work experience under their belts. "Many have only operated in an environment where people told them what to do," Keith said. "They're now thrust into a situation where there's often no right answer. Succeeding in this environment requires a big mindset shift."

This is the time to dig in, and not give up. Things will get better as you get better. There is likely a gap between who you are and who you want to become. The way to bridge this gap is to develop the skill set and mindset necessary to succeed. Muscles only grow after they are broken down by strenuous exercise. Your mind works this way, too. Place yourself under stress and force yourself to grow. Push yourself to the limit of what you think you're capable of and then push past that. This rigor is what's required to have a growth mindset, and having a growth mindset is critical to becoming an Essential Associate.

An Essential Summary and Action Steps

1. Many lawyers are hyper-focused on achieving future milestones like making partner and earning enough money to retire. This leads them to be unhappy in the moment and fixated on the future. The problem is that the future isn't necessarily better, just different.

2. Young lawyers struggle because they don't learn to love (or at least like) the day-to-day process of the practice of law. The passion they thought they had for the law (often based on popular culture distortions of what it's like to be a lawyer) wanes once the realities of the profession sink in. For a person who embraces the process, each day isn't drudgery; it's another opportunity for fulfillment. Partnership becomes a goal, but not an obsession, because there is satisfaction in the everyday.

3. Take solace in knowing that as you grow and get better, satisfaction will follow. You can't "find" passion. You must develop it over time. If you build mastery, then you'll come to appreciate and be fulfilled by your work and the independence and rewards that come with it. If you can buy into the idea of "cultivating" and "developing" passion, as opposed to "finding" or "following" it, then this mindset can arm you with the understanding that you can work toward building more passion for your job. Successful lawyers manage to find passion in what they do, which allows them to do more of it—faster, better, and for longer—than their peers.

4. Any time you're learning a new skill, or building something worthwhile, it's hard. Enjoyment only comes after you've practiced enough to acquire a high level of skill. You can't just follow your

passion and expect that to be enough. When engaging in a challenging career, mastery is almost always a precursor to passion. And if you want to gain mastery of the practice of law, you have to practice, practice, practice.

5. The type of practice you engage in is critical—you can't just go through the motions and expect to get better. Deliberate practice is purposeful, systematic, and requires focused attention; it's conducted with the specific goal of improving performance. It's work that stretches you beyond your current abilities. If you're engaged in deliberate practice, it means you're deeply immersed in your work. Young lawyers who incorporate the principles of deliberate practice into their legal careers plan their work thoughtfully, work intensely on it, and then seek feedback from others on their performance.

6. A young lawyer who embraces the concept of deliberate practice is one that has a growth mindset, and is motivated by challenges and sees failure as an opportunity. Lawyers with growth mindsets believe they can get better through experience. Most successful people have growth mindsets. Having a growth mindset is almost a prerequisite for someone to succeed in a difficult profession, such as the practice of law, because every challenging endeavor involves failure and setbacks that require resilience.

6

Seek Balance

"In the long run, we shape our lives, and we shape ourselves. The process never ends until we die. And, the choices we make are ultimately our own responsibility."

– ELEANOR ROOSEVELT

I n 1955, Cyril Northcote Parkinson, a British historian, wrote an essay in *The Economist* in which he described a phenomenon that would come to be called "Parkinson's Law." He wrote: "Work expands so as to fill the time available for its completion." If something must be done in a day, it will get done in a day. If something must be done in a year, it will get done in a year.

If you believe that achieving success as an associate takes 3,000 hours of work per year, then it will. It's Parkinson's Law of being a lawyer. Working hard, working long hours, working late into the night—too many of us accept the inevitability of a life driven primarily by work, and interspersed with brief interludes of quality personal time.

Many lawyers fill the vacuum of their available time with work, and as a result work more hours than they need to. There are many reasons for this. Some think it's expected of them, and others just don't have a good handle on their days. Still others adopt workaholism as a persona.

Let's face it, for most of us work is not fun. It can and should be satisfying, and your passion for the profession can grow, but it's not a hobby. Work should *serve life*, not *be life*. The belief that the only way to build a successful legal practice is to give everything to it is a myth. For most this is the path to burnout and dissatisfaction, or even health problems.

If you want to become an Essential Associate and experience success over the long-term, you need to find some semblance of balance now, and not hope for it later. Otherwise, the job will own you instead of you owning your job. You can give everything to a legal career and achieve success (depending on what your definition of "success" is), but living a truly rich life requires a more balanced approach.

CRAFT A SCHEDULE THAT WORKS FOR YOU AND SET ASIDE TIME TO DECOMPRESS

It's indisputable that due to hefty billable hour requirements, and expectations that associates be at the beck and call of partners and clients, law firms contribute to work/life balance problems in the profession. But law firms are not solely, and perhaps not even primarily, to blame. For many associates, the lack of work/life balance is a self-inflicted wound.

A recent survey by the Diversity & Flexibility Alliance found that while more law firms are offering perks and programs intended to enable associates to work more flexible schedules, such as the ability to work remotely and work fewer hours in return for less compensation, only eight percent of associates take advantage of these programs.

A knee-jerk response to this statistic would be to argue: "Yes, but the reason most associates aren't taking advantage of these programs is a fear of being penalized by their law firms when it comes time for bonuses and advancement." But as it turns out, more law firms seem to be increasingly open-minded when it comes to the issue of flexible work schedules. Fourteen of the twenty-eight firms participating in the Diversity & Flexibility Alliance survey promoted at least one lawyer working a reduced schedule to partner in 2015, which is twice as many as in 2014. Twelve of the twenty-eight firms also reported having lawyers working reduced schedules in their leadership ranks, including three chairs or managing partners, eleven department chairs or practice group leaders, and four office heads.

While these types of statistics are heartening, it's important to not read too much into them. The quickest and surest path to mastery and partnership is not by working part-time and from home. Consistent hard work and focus over the long-term is required. But that does not mean you should operate at a full sprint all of the time. You need to give your mind and body the opportunity to rest and recover throughout your career.

Think about your legal career the way top athletes think about theirs. They work in intervals, with bouts of intense training followed by periods of rest and recovery. Building recovery time into training is important because it is during periods of rest that the body adapts to the stress of exercise and grows stronger. Recovery allows the body to replenish energy and repair damaged tissues and muscles. It's when athletes train too hard, for too long, that they get injured.

The same is true of how you must work as a lawyer. It can't be all intensity all of the time. If your goal is to make partner at a law firm some years from now, look ahead and figure out how to build time for recovery into your schedule. You need to take care of your mind and your body if you want them to function at the peak levels required to be a top performer. When you're working, work hard. When you're not, detach. Take a long-term approach to your career. If you look at each day in isolation, you'll tend to sprint and burn out. If you have a long-term view, you'll run a slow, methodical marathon and cover much more ground as a result.

> "When you become a lawyer at a law firm it's easy for it to become all-encompassing. You need to remember that you are still a person with outside interests who should pursue them. Don't give them up. This is a marathon, not a sprint."
> — SCOTT WOLFSON, PARTNER AT WOLFSON BOLTON

It's unrealistic to expect that your life will always be in balance. There will be busy times, and there will be times that are a bit less busy. The key to achieving some semblance of balance is to be thoughtful and purposeful about scheduling time for yourself and for loved ones.

Take vacations to get away, rest, and introduce interesting new stimulus and experiences into your existence. Use flexible schedules to bridge gaps in your career during particularly challenging periods of time in life, such as the birth of a child or when you have to care for a sick parent. It accomplishes nothing—for you, your clients, or your firm—if you continue head down through these challenges while not taking a moment, or even months, if necessary, to decompress and recharge.

EXERCISE, SLEEP, AND BE MINDFUL

As a young lawyer, you know what it's like to sit at a desk for most of your waking hours. You understand how easy it is to eat lots of take-out food out of convenience. Perhaps you've gone through a period of having a few drinks after work to take the edge off. Be careful. It's easy to get into an unhealthy routine—far easier than it is to get back into a healthy one.

Be mindful of your health. Get up from your desk to take a brisk walk. Schedule your workout before work, because it's easy for your day to get away from you, and your post-work spinning class will be the first thing to get bumped on your to-do list. Get in the habit of eating a healthy breakfast, because lunch and dinner may be consumed at your desk or in a conference room out of a Styrofoam container.

Prioritize sleep. According to the American Academy of Sleep Medicine, routinely sleeping fewer than seven hours a night can result in "adverse health outcomes, including weight gain and obesity, diabetes, hypertension, heart disease and stroke, depression, and increased risk of death." While good health should be reason enough to get more sleep, numerous studies have found that sleep deprivation also significantly impacts your ability to focus and perform cognitively demanding work. Sleep will be hard to come by, but find ways to prioritize it. It can be your secret weapon over the course of a long career.

Lawyers and other top professionals in fields such as technology and finance are increasingly turning to mindfulness practices such as meditation to help them through the stress of their days. Meditation increases mindfulness and helps you to stay in the present moment, rather than worrying about the implications of past decisions or feeling anxiety about the future. Meditation doesn't require a yoga mat and sounds of whales singing—just take a short walk and focus on your movements and breathing. When you're feeling stressed, a little mindfulness can pull you out of a negative mental spiral and recognize the stress for what it is, which is a moment in time that you can transcend, just as you've done before.

Bottom-line: Take care of yourself.

DON'T DRINK TOO MUCH

Friday happy hour. Summer program socials. Practice group dinners. Celebratory client dinners. Late nights in the office. It's Thursday. There are many occasions to drink while working at a law firm, which helps explain why heavy drinking is a problem for so many lawyers.

The American Bar Association conducted a sobering study (pun intended) about the incidence of problem drinking and mental health issues among lawyers. According to the study:

- Twenty-one percent of attorneys are problem drinkers
- Twenty-eight percent struggle with some level of depression
- Nineteen percent demonstrate symptoms of anxiety
- Younger attorneys in the first ten years of practice exhibit the highest incidence of problems

While these statistics are dramatic and worth sharing, not much needs to be said about them. You're smart and you know the problems caused by habitual alcohol consumption.

For many young associates, the type of drinking that will lead to trouble is not habitual drinking done at a bar or at home, but casual, social drinking that takes place at firm events and results in regretful behavior. Alcohol flows freely at most firm events, but it should go without saying that a firm function is not the right venue to blow off steam. You don't want your name to pop up in a story on Above the Law lest you become an anecdote in the annals of young associate career implosion.

I had a few close calls early in my career, some as a summer associate and others as a first or second-year lawyer. I think that my lapses in judgment as a summer associate resulted from hubris, whereas those as a young associate resulted from moments of fatigue, stress, and stupidity.

Have fun but choose the occasions to do so wisely. When in doubt, set a two-drink maximum for yourself. Order a glass of soda or sparkling water on the rocks. Make a point not to finish the mixed drink your colleague ordered for you. Don't let the waiter keep refilling your wine glass at the dinner table. You can still "act the part" and network with partners, clients, and colleagues at social functions without putting yourself at risk by consuming too much alcohol. Have a good time, but be careful, because there are few ways to torpedo your reputation more quickly than being the drunk associate at a firm function.

DEVELOP OUTSIDE INTERESTS

If you're going to enjoy your job enough to put in the long hours required to get ahead then you need to have something to look forward to outside of the office to act as a counterbalance. In fact, outside interests aren't just helpful distractions from the rigors of work; they can help fuel a successful career.

One of the most common refrains from those who insist that outside interests and the practice of law are incompatible is that there is not enough time to pursue both. But there's always time—you just need to set priorities and accept the trade-offs.

Take Amelia Boone, for example. She's a corporate lawyer at Apple and previously was an associate at Skadden, Arps, Slate, Meagher & Flom. She's also a world-class endurance athlete and has won a number of brutal obstacle races, including the World's Toughest Mudder, the Spartan world title, and Vermont's Death Races. She didn't start training or racing until after she became an associate at Skadden. Her colleagues convinced her to sign up for her first Tough Mudder.

In an interview, Boone discussed how she endures the grueling schedule required to race and practice law, which involves waking up at 4 a.m. to train in the wee hours of the morning. She explained that getting up early to train is the trade-off that allows her to pursue two things she loves at the same time and at the highest levels.

Crawling through barbed-wire, running through semi-frozen pools of water, and climbing up ropes and hurdling over walls may not be *your thing*, but it's important to find *a thing* and carve out time for it.

Young lawyers should focus on developing and pursuing outside interests early in their careers. Humans are creatures of habit, and if your habit is work, then it will become harder to break the habit as you progress in your career. Find something outside of the office that you love and can't wait to get back to, which will lead you to become more efficient and effective with your time in the office.

BE CAREFUL ABOUT YOUR FINANCES

Money doesn't buy happiness but it sure can cause stress. As a young attorney fresh out of law school, you will likely be making more money than you ever have—way more.

I graduated from law school in 2001. Shortly before I started as a summer associate at Skadden, between my second and third years of law school, New York firms announced a big bump in associate salaries. This was in the midst of the tech bubble and massive run-up in the stock markets. Most firms moved first-year salaries up to $125,000. Skadden went up to $140,000.

I thought I was going to be rich.

Don't get me wrong, it was an astonishing amount of money, especially for someone like me who grew up in a middle-class household and whose previous earning experience was limited to summer jobs in restaurants and retail. However, I learned quickly that there are two sides to the ledger. Financial security requires a focus on earning and spending.

It's a simple lesson to learn, but not an easy one to put into practice: Don't overspend. Just don't.

Most of the stuff you buy won't make you happy. It won't make things easier. It won't make people perceive you differently. Don't make spending—be it on cars, clothes, or expensive vacations—a form of stress relief. If you're not careful, you can become addicted to a high level of income, which will foreclose options to make changes in the future.

There may come a day when you decide to start a company, move to the prosecutor's office, go back to school, travel the world, start a blog, or stay home with your kids. Don't let poor financial decisions made early in your career keep you from pursuing a different path. The job of a lawyer is stressful enough. Don't add money woes to the mix.

BE GRATEFUL AND CELEBRATE THE SMALL WINS

You are in an environment full of smart people. Many of the lawyers around you are financially successful. There are lots of fancy clothes, expensive cars, and other trappings of success on display.

It's easy to get caught up in this and start to play the comparison game. Rather than being grateful for your fortunate circumstances—a good paying, relatively secure job with lots of upside potential—there's often a tendency to fixate on what others have that you don't.

This is a recipe for discontent. If you can shift your mindset from one of envy to one of gratitude, you'll find it much easier to be happy. One of the best ways to add contentment and happiness to your day is to celebrate small wins. Your days will be full of struggle, but also progress.

Teresa Amabile and Steven Kramer explored the importance of celebrating successes in a 2011 article in the *Harvard Business Review* called "The Power of Small Wins." In it, Amabile and Kramer describe the importance of the "progress principle," which relates to the positive emotional and motivational boost that people enjoy from making progress in meaningful work.

To harness the power of the progress principle, lawyers need to recognize incremental achievements each day, week, and month. Progress in any complex legal matter is slow, and if all one focuses on is the outcome, then it's hard to derive much satisfaction from the day-to-day grind.

Maintain the proper perspective. Be grateful for your circumstances. As tough as things may seem at the moment, they could be far worse. Take time each day to celebrate a small win or two.

An Essential Summary and Action Steps

1. If you want to become an Essential Associate and experience success over the long-term, you need to find some semblance of balance now, and not hope for it later. Otherwise, the job will own you instead of you owning your job. You can give everything to a legal career and achieve success (depending on what your definition of "success" is), but living a truly rich life requires a more balanced approach.

2. Think about your legal career the way top athletes think about theirs. They work in intervals, with bouts of intense training followed by periods of rest and recovery. This allows their bodies to adapt to the stress of exercise and grow stronger. The same is true of how you must work as a lawyer. It can't be all intensity all of the time. If your goal is to make partner at a law firm some years from now, look ahead and figure out how to build time for recovery into your schedule. You need to take care of your mind and your body if you want them to function at the peak levels required to be a top performer. If you don't, you'll burn out.

3. As a busy, young lawyer, it's easy to get into an unhealthy routine— far easier than it is to get back into a healthy one. Schedule time for exercise. Prioritize sleep. Adopt a mindfulness practice. Not only will this improve your health, but it will improve your performance as well.

4. Limit your alcohol consumption, especially at networking and client events, which are anxiety-inducing environments. It's easy to

fall back on a few drinks to take the edge off, but if you consume too much, you're setting yourself up for problems. Have a plan going in—set a two-drink limit for yourself.

5. A legal career can become all-encompassing if you let it. Find something—a hobby, interest, or activity—outside of the office and carve out time for it. Humans are creatures of habit, and if your habit is work, then it will become harder to break the habit as you progress in your career. When you find something you love outside of work, you'll become more efficient and effective with your time in the office.

6. Don't increase your stress, complicate your life, and reduce your options by overspending.

7. Take time to appreciate all of the hard work you're putting in. Don't expect anyone else to recognize your achievements, so be mindful of the progress you're making, and celebrate your small wins.

PART II

STAND OUT

EXCEL IN THE BUSINESS
OF LAW

7

Create a Foundation for Future Business Development

―――――

"I will prepare and some day my chance will come."

― ABRAHAM LINCOLN

S cott Becker is a Harvard Law School graduate and a partner at McGuireWoods, where he previously served as the chair of the firm's healthcare practice group. Early in his career, he realized that to get control over his life, and direction over his practice, he needed clients of his own. He was "intent on building something."

When he was a young associate, Scott began looking around to see how other lawyers in his firm that he admired and respected, and who had built practices themselves, went about the process. He discovered commonalities and found a mentor who was willing to help.

His mentor, also a healthcare lawyer, urged him to carve out a niche. Scott realized that having a niche would mean working with clients with similar problems, and he would be able to build his expertise in a specific area and offer it to those similarly situated.

Scott knew that clients weren't going to appear on his doorstep if he didn't put in some hard work to attract them, so he tried different marketing tactics. According to Scott, "There is no perfect plan. You need to experiment to figure out what works."

Scott realized that as a young lawyer he would need to have a long-term approach to building a practice. "You can't aim straight for the top," Scott said. "It's almost impossible to compete with big firms who are investing huge resources into protecting their biggest clients. But there are lots of smaller clients in niche industries that you can pursue. As you build up your practice and your expertise, then later in your career you'll be in a position to go after the bigger clients. You need to hit singles and doubles before you can hit home runs."

With the support of his firm, Scott identified three potential niche areas within the healthcare industry that were underserved but had potential and began pursuing work. He drew upon the principles of a business book he read early in his career that emphasized the importance of "getting in the middle" of an industry. Heeding that lesson, Scott created newsletters geared to each niche audience and began hosting small industry conferences. He started gaining traction serving surgical centers, and once his direction was clear he poured all of his energy into it.

He was intent on building a practice but didn't want to be the guy that was trying to sell to his friends and family. "If I was going to be in it for the long haul, I knew I needed to create a marketing and business development platform that was going to be sustainable and reach more broadly than my inner circle," Scott said.

Scott realized that if he wanted to build a sustainable practice he needed to get himself and his expertise in front of as many potential clients as frequently as possible. He created and disseminated useful information to industry leaders. He engaged in content marketing before that term became part of marketing lexicon.

His newsletter became widely read, and he became widely known. As a result, he started to develop lots of business. After he became known as an expert in his surgical center niche, larger opportunities with hospitals and health systems emerged.

But he never stopped doing what got him there, which was staying in the middle of his target industry. What started as a newsletter grew into Becker's Healthcare, one of the most widely read and respected healthcare publishing platforms in the world. It's now a successful business itself, and it's also a big part of what continues to drive Scott's legal practice.

To what does Scott attribute his success? He built his personal brand within a niche industry and stuck with it, which allowed him to serve larger clients within the industry over time. Scott believes that many associates lack a long-term commitment when starting the process of building a brand and a practice. "It takes a tremendous amount of effort," Scott said. "You need to constantly be in front of your audience providing personalized content. Most lawyers don't get results quickly enough, so they don't stick with it. Building a practice is a serious job, a full-time job, and you need to treat it as such."

It's hard for young associates to have this sort of long-term perspective early in their careers. As we discussed previously, associates often hear mixed messages about the importance of working to build a practice from day one. There is merit to the idea that associates should prioritize gaining mastery of the practice of law, first and foremost. Indeed, nothing else really matters until you've developed good judgment, effective communication skills, and a high, if not yet expert, level of skill in your chosen area of practice.

But then what? There was a time when putting your head down and "doing good work" for someone else's clients was enough for lawyers to advance in their careers. Clients were institutional, and business development expectations were much different. In today's legal marketplace, that's no longer the case. The economics have changed. Firms can't freely bill for junior associate time. Gone are the days when associates inherited institutional client work as they advanced toward partner. Now, more than ever, associates must start laying a foundation for future business development very early in the careers—not after they've focused on gaining mastery over the practice of law, but at the same time.

Having clients is important for many reasons. A loyal stable of clients is the most valuable form of career currency that a lawyer can have. Not only is a lawyer with clients a valued asset in their own firm, but they are attractive to others as well. Clients create leverage for lawyers. At most firms, having a book of business (or at least demonstrating a strong ability to develop one) is a requirement to make partner. It increases one's compensation. It's intrinsically satisfying in that clients, by spending their hard-earned money, validate your own hard work. Most importantly, it's empowering. Having clients allows a lawyer to have a greater semblance of control over their career and personal life.

According to a report by *The Journal of Personality and Social Psychology*, "autonomy," defined as "the feeling that your life—its activities and habits—are self-chosen and self-endorsed," is the highest predictor of happiness among people. Money? Popularity? Good looks? Nope. Autonomy trumps them all. The desire to gain control is what motivated Scott Becker, and many other successful lawyers, to build a practice. One of the few ways to have autonomy in a law firm is to have clients of your own.

That's not to say that having clients is easy. It creates a whole new set of pressures and responsibilities. When you own the client relationship you own the ultimate responsibility to produce excellent work and provide exceptional client service to maintain the relationship.

But in a choice between the alternatives of having or not having a book of business, having clients gives you far more options. Lawyers who desire more control over their lives and careers will likely never get it if they're dependent on others for billable hours. Without clients, a lawyer's time and compensation are reliant upon, and subject to the whims of, colleagues with books of business. If you have clients, you'll make more money, have more options, and have more autonomy over your career destiny.

If building a profitable book of business is so important, then how come so few lawyers, young and old, prioritize it, let alone accomplish it? The problem is not one of knowledge; most of us know what we need to be doing. It's not one of desire; most lawyers want the benefits that come with building a book of business. The problem is one of action. We equivocate and procrastinate despite knowing how important it is for us to act.

Because it's easier to procrastinate than it is to take action, we grasp on to things we have heard, read, and come to believe that lead us to put off the hard work that we should be doing today until some undetermined point in the future.

When it comes to building a practice, we tell ourselves: I can start later.

As a young associate, it's likely been drilled into your head that your most important responsibilities are to work hard, bill lots of hours, and do high-quality work. This is true. These things must be your focus. A problem only arises if you focus on nothing else, like laying a foundation for future business development. Therefore, old-school advice that suggests that all you need to worry about now is becoming a good lawyer, and business development will take care of itself later, can serve as what author Jon Acuff calls a "noble obstacle." A noble obstacle is something you do, or tell yourself, that seems important and productive, but in reality is impeding you from achieving your priorities.

This type of thinking gets young lawyers into trouble a few years down the road. From day one, you need to be aware that each stage in your legal career is like a season. Things are always changing around you, and you can never stand still. The day you make partner is not the time to start thinking about business development. In fact, this day may never come if this is your approach. Nor is it when you reach the midpoint in your progression as an associate, when you start hearing the phrase "partnership track" used during annual reviews. It's now. If you want to build a book of business and make partner at a law firm, you need to start acting with a sense of urgency.

> ## "Business development is a ten to fifteen-year process, so get started early."
> — DALJIT DOOGAL, PARTNER AT FOLEY & LARDNER

If you plan to make this your profession, know this: At some point, you'll wake up and realize that you need to build a practice and wish you had started sooner. Business development is not a faucet that you can turn on and off when you please. There's an old Chinese proverb that says, "The best time to plant a tree was twenty years ago. The next best time is today." When it comes to building a practice, start today.

As a young associate at a law firm it's unrealistic to think that you'll be bringing in much, if any, actual client work until you've gained more experience and expertise. But it's even more unrealistic to think that you'll bring in work later if you don't plant the seeds of business development—things like building a network, building a name for yourself, and building a platform to share your ideas—if you don't begin right now.

So how do you take control of your career and become an Essential Associate? It's almost always ideal to work on one thing at a time with undivided focus. But you're operating in the real world, not an ideal one, so you have adjust. In this game, to excel and gain autonomy, you need to master both the practice and the business of law. Therefore, instead of simply being a lawyer, focus from day one on building a practice. You may not have the ability or opportunity to bring in clients at this stage of your career, but nothing is stopping you from taking the necessary steps now to put yourself in the best position possible to develop business later. Part Two of this book lays out a step-by-step guide to create a foundation for future business development, which is best accomplished by building a powerful personal brand. If you want to stand out, you need to get started.

Putting Ideas into Action

To help you take action on the ideas addressed in Part Two of this book, I created the "90-Day Personal Brand Building Road Map," which is available to purchase and download on my website at www.TheEssentialAssociate.com, and www.attorneyatwork.com.

The 90-Day Road Map will help you to identify your weaknesses and showcase your strengths so that you can effectively communicate your personal brand to the marketplace. It builds on the lessons taught in this book and will help you to both create and implement a plan to build your brand. The ninety-day timeframe is not to suggest that building a personal brand takes ninety days. The truth is you never stop building a brand. The purpose is to get you moving, and racking up small wins so that you have the momentum to keep moving forward.

8

The Power of a Personal Brand

"Always be a first-rate version of yourself and not a second-rate version of someone else."

– JUDY GARLAND

The problem with most business development advice is that it's tactical and not strategic. Do this. Don't do that. Try this software. Dabble in that social media platform. Tactics are important but only in the context of a larger strategy. And the ultimate strategy for a young lawyer hoping to build a sustainable business development pipeline is to build a strong personal brand.

There's no great dictionary definition of the term "personal brand." Trying to define personal branding is like Justice Potter Stewart trying to define "obscenity"—you know it when you see it. Take a look around at others in your firm. There are partners, and perhaps even some associates, with strong brands among your ranks. These are lawyers who get calls from members of the media. They generate lots of speaking opportunities. They garner attention not (or at least not only) for their outsized personalities, but rather for their outsized expertise in a particular practice area or industry.

One of the most frequently cited colloquial definitions of branding is from Amazon CEO Jeff Bezos, who said, "Your brand is what people say about you when you're not in the room." Put another way, a personal brand is what sells you when you're not there to sell yourself. It's the natural result of your behavior in the marketplace.

There are three steps required to build a strong personal brand:

1. Choose a narrow niche market to serve

2. Create awareness and build your reputation in your niche market

3. Grow, cultivate, and nourish relationships over time

Building a strong personal brand is not a passive endeavor. As we will discuss in detail in the chapters to come, it's an active process that takes time, patience, and lots of hard work. The process is what's required to identify a target market, capture attention, build relationships, and establish trust that will lead to future business development opportunities. The odds are that your law firm invests heavily in building its brand. There are a number of reasons that you need to focus on building your personal brand as well.

IT'S A WAY TO SCALE YOURSELF

You're likely familiar with the concept of "scale" in business. We see it all of the time in the tech world, where startups work furiously to scale up and build infrastructure to manage and absorb growth when the time comes.

Businesses can scale, but can people? It's an issue that many lawyers and other professional services providers struggle with. You're one person with tremendous demands on your time due to the needs of your clients, colleagues, and firm (not to mention your personal life). You can't be everywhere at once, which limits your ability to grow your book of business. If you're taking a deposition, you can't also be taking a client to lunch.

This is a problem because business development in professional services is still an intensely personal endeavor. You need to be out there, meeting people, developing and spreading your reputation among potential clients and referral sources. It takes time and energy, which are both resources in short supply for most lawyers. You can't clone yourself, so your ability to scale yourself is limited. You can't be everywhere, focused on everything all at once.

Or can you?

After all, it's not necessarily your physical presence that matters when it comes to building your reputation among buyers of legal services. More important is the power of your ideas, and word-of-mouth marketing from people who know and trust you. If your ideas gain traction and spread among your audience, then you can still make an impact on someone regardless of whether you can engage with them one-on-one. Accordingly, it is possible to scale yourself if you focus on growing your personal brand.

A personal brand is a promise. It clarifies and communicates what makes you unique. Crafting this promise requires you to understand your values and strengths. It also requires self-awareness. It's important to know your weaknesses, too.

Once you know who you are, and what you have to offer, then you can spread this message in the marketplace of ideas through the articles you write, the speeches you give, how you position yourself on social media and your firm bio page, what organizations you're involved with, what causes you support, who you associate with, and the manner in which you present yourself in other public settings.

You, as an individual limited by the laws of physics, are not scalable. But your personal brand and the promise of value you project into the marketplace can spread and grow.

IT CREATES ALIGNMENT BETWEEN YOUR EXPERTISE AND A CLIENT'S NEEDS

Your personal brand is impacted and shaped by everything you do, and don't do, to put your best foot forward. If clients are going to buy from you, they need to understand who you are, what you stand for, and the value you bring to the table.

Sure, some clients buy sight unseen, but that rarely leads to a relationship that lasts over time. The most meaningful, satisfying, and profitable engagements typically result from situations where clients seek out a specific lawyer for a particular reason. They know who they are looking for and why, have done their due diligence, and often have been referred to the lawyer by someone they trust. There's clear alignment between what the client needs and what the lawyer has to offer.

The only way for them to know that there's alignment—as opposed to just hiring someone and hoping for the best—is if the lawyer projects a powerful personal brand into the marketplace. A lawyer with a strong personal brand puts prospective clients at ease because they can more directly discern what the lawyer does, and how and why they do it.

By serving clients within a specific niche, you'll be better equipped to understand what problems your clients face. If you can identify and articulate those problems, you'll be in a position to communicate with members of your audience in a way that resonates.

Putting the work in to become a well-branded lawyer offering specific solutions to a particular audience is worth the effort. Once you define what you do and for whom, you won't have to chase as much business. It will start chasing you.

IT HELPS TO OVERCOME BUYER'S REMORSE

Think about your own past experiences trying to hire someone to help out with an issue. It's hard, right? Hiring a service provider, be it a carpenter or a lawyer, is difficult because you're making a commitment in advance based on someone's promise to deliver a result in the future. It's not like "kicking the tires" on a product before a purchase.

Before committing to someone you probably felt a certain level of unease. You asked yourself: "Does this person know what they are doing? Is the price fair? Will they do what they say? Will they complete the task on time and on budget?"

Anxiety grows when the service provider starts using platitudes to describe their alleged expertise, and making vague claims and using jargon to illustrate the problem and proposed solution. This is meant to impress you, but it only frustrates and confuses you.

On the other hand, a service provider who communicates a calm and measured description of their expertise, experience, and approach to solving the problem increases your confidence that you are speaking to the right person. You focus less on price than you would have if you still felt unsure about the person's abilities. After all, you likely care more about the outcome than you do the cost, and you're probably willing to pay a bit more if you trust that the problem will be addressed the first time correctly, without having to go through the process again.

New business engagements of any variety that begin well, with high levels of mutual trust and respect, tend to end well. A distinct and compelling personal brand helps to overcome buyer's remorse. A personal brand helps clients take the leap of faith required to hire a lawyer, and move forward with a higher level of confidence.

IT'S A WAY TO TELL A COMPELLING STORY

Building a strong personal brand is no easy task. It's comforting to think that we understand what our personal brand says about us, but when we take a more in-depth look, it's easy to see the fallacy in that logic. Your personal brand isn't what you say or think it is. As Jeff Bezos said, it's reflected in what other people say about you.

Your personal brand is the story people use to describe you to others; and it's far better if the story is one you crafted, instead of one conjured up by someone else.

Hundreds, and perhaps thousands, of other lawyers do what you do. As much as you'd like to believe it, it's highly unlikely that you have a unique skill set. But you do have a collection of values, life, and work experiences that make you unique. In this sense, you do offer something of value that no one else can offer: a set of skills filtered through your lens on the world.

You have a story to tell. And if your personal brand reflects your personal story, members of your audience will know who you are, what you stand for, your professional strengths, and what they can expect when they hire you.

Think about how many times you've been asked what you do for a living, or what practice area you're in, and eyes have glazed over at your answer. How many networking events have you been at where you begin describing your background and the person you're speaking with begins to tune out? How many people read your website bio or LinkedIn profile from start to finish, let alone engage with it? Do you leave a positive impression, and a memorable mark, after any of these interactions? If not, why not?

Developing your personal brand story doesn't mean being boastful. A well-defined brand lets people know who you are and what you do. They'll understand your strengths, the value you provide, and the types of situations you're uniquely qualified to handle. By focusing on crafting a powerful personal brand, you'll have a powerful story to tell. Yes, a lawyer's personal brand is a story. If it's a gripping tale, it can lead to the type of word-of-mouth that sells your services, even when you're not there to sell them yourself.

IT'S A CODE TO LIVE BY

Think about your network of friends and colleagues, and what first comes to mind when you consider each person within your network. There are probably a few people who immediately come to mind who you would call if you were ever in a tight spot. These people are dependable. There may be others you would reach out to after experiencing difficulty or loss. These people are empathetic. Others may be on speed-dial if you have a home improvement project to complete. These people are resourceful. The reason that you associate these people with particular attributes is that they have reinforced these qualities through their actions over time. People are drawn to others not because of the beliefs they hold, but rather because of the consistency of their beliefs, as manifested by their actions.

What comes to mind when members of your network think of you? What is the code you live by? What is the personal attribute that you are known for? Developing a powerful personal brand requires a heavy dose of self-awareness. Are you generous? Are you hardworking? Are you reliable? Assess and understand your unique strengths, and then build your brand by reinforcing your key personal attributes through all of the actions you take and the relationships you form.

IT BUILDS BRIDGES TO BUSINESS DEVELOPMENT

Personal branding and business development are distinct concepts, but also inextricably linked in important ways. Business development in the legal industry is a long game played over many years, and the key to building a sustainable book of business is accomplished, first, by building a strong personal brand.

Scott Becker didn't begin his quest to build a practice by knocking on doors and making cold calls to potential clients asking for business. He worked hard to develop his reputation as a thought leader and build his network within a narrow industry. He began crafting his personal brand while he was still an associate, and then he generated business development opportunities as a result of his efforts. He had to take the first step before he could take the second and expect any success. This is the approach of someone who's playing the long game.

A short-term approach to business development, on the other hand, requires the hard sell. The hard sell approach is a central theme in the classic movie *Glengarry Glen Ross*, in which Alec Baldwin's infamous character, Blake, admonishes a group of real estate salesmen to "ABC," which is an acronym for "Always Be Closing."

Whether it's at the local car dealership or electronics superstore, we all deal with salespeople who take the ABC hard-sell approach. Sometimes it even works, especially when what's being sold is a commodity or some other inexpensive product or service that we might need on the spur of the moment. Despite the salesperson's off-putting approach, we buy because it's convenient to do so at the moment; or we just want to get the person off the phone or off the front porch.

An "always be closing" approach may work well for salespeople in certain industries, but it almost never works when it comes to business development in the legal industry. This is because the precursor to legal engagements is mutual trust between attorney and client, and trust can only be built over time. If you try to close the deal with a prospective new client too early, then trust and goodwill will evaporate—along with the opportunity. By positioning yourself as the expert and demonstrating that you understand and can solve the types of problems that your clients face, it allows people to sell themselves on the idea of hiring you. A strong personal brand builds a bridge to business development.

IS IT WORKING?

Let's say you've bought into the benefits of developing a personal brand, and have taken the steps outlined in the next several chapters meant to guide you in building your own. Here are some of the benefits that you can expect.

1. Other attorneys and professionals will take notice, and better understand what you do. You'll receive more referrals aligned with your expertise, and less that aren't.

2. Clients, too. As with referral sources, clients and prospective clients will have a better sense of your expertise. They'll know what you do and how you can help, and new opportunities will reflect that understanding.

3. You'll be more visible. Because you are a more focused and visible expert in your niche, both online and offline, your content marketing efforts will become sharper and more valuable. Your ideas will attract more ears and eyeballs and new opportunities to speak and write will present themselves.

4. You'll be more profitable. One of the key factors that drives down prices in any market is the availability of substitutes. As a well-branded expert, your expertise will be perceived as rare and valuable, which will enable you to charge more for your services.

5. You'll be more productive. Once you narrow your focus and direct your energy, you'll increase your productivity. More importantly, your productivity will be geared toward a clear objective. You'll feel less scattered because you'll no longer be trying to serve and please everyone.

6. At a minimum, you'll be more purposeful. Many of us approach our careers without a plan and drift from day to day, then year to year. By focusing on developing a powerful personal brand, you'll have something to aspire to, and benchmark against, on a consistent basis.

9

Essential Step One: Choose a Niche

"It is not enough to be busy; so are the ants. The question is: What are we busy about?"

– HENRY DAVID THOREAU

I n the Introduction to this book, I mentioned that I started a law firm in Detroit as a relatively young lawyer. I took the plunge in early 2009 at the height of the financial crisis, on the cusp of the automotive crisis, and just a couple of years before Detroit's municipal bankruptcy filing. Given the impending bankruptcies of General Motors and Chrysler, I knew that there would be lots of restructuring work available in my practice area niche, but I figured I would have more success if I could define an even narrower focus.

Rather than trying to position myself as a generalist within the corporate bankruptcy practice area, I decided to target automotive dealerships, which occupy a much smaller and under-appreciated vertical within the automotive industry. Auto dealers are an integral part of the automotive supply chain, but there were so many $100 million-and-up businesses that needed help figuring out how to deal with the looming bankruptcies of two of their largest customers, there was little attention focused on Detroit's many $5-$50 million auto dealers.

I didn't make this decision haphazardly. Because most of the large law firms in Detroit represented the "Big Three" auto manufacturers in some capacity or another, I anticipated that there would be conflict referral work that needed to be done for these firms' auto supplier clients. But I didn't want to be dependent on these referrals, so I decided to pursue a strategy within a niche that larger firms either ignored or were uncompetitive in due to price.

Before diving in with auto dealers, I conducted an assessment of my strengths and evaluated opportunities within my network. During the years preceding my decision to start my firm, I had developed relationships with auto dealer attorneys at a firm that I had done work for as a marketing consultant. They had a roster of auto dealer clients, and I had experience in corporate bankruptcy proceedings that they did not, so it seemed like a good fit.

I supplemented my networking with writing and speaking for the local auto dealers association related to the potential impact of Big Three automotive bankruptcy filings. This allowed me to expand my network beyond attorneys to the actual operators in the space. This led to years' worth of significant work in the General Motors and Chrysler bankruptcies, and the federal arbitration proceedings that came next for dealers whose franchise agreements were terminated during the bankruptcies.

This didn't happen by accident. It resulted from a strategic decision to get narrow within a niche.

THE IMPORTANCE OF ESTABLISHING A NICHE

The first step in building a personal brand that will lead to future business development opportunities is accepting that you can't serve everyone. To succeed in today's competitive environment and knowledge economy, you need to offer the marketplace something different in the form of narrow, specialized expertise.

It's not that being a well-rounded lawyer is a bad thing. A lawyer with depth and breadth of knowledge is a valuable asset to a client. The problem is that positioning oneself as providing "full service" or possessing "general knowledge" is often ineffective from a brand positioning standpoint. Lawyers who cast a wide net believe that if they chase the biggest market possible then they'll have a better opportunity to acquire more clients. But most quickly learn that the opposite is true. You can't be all things to all people and expect to make an impact.

Having a niche allows you to communicate your value proposition to a distinct and highly targeted market. Your message can be more relevant and better contextualized for your specific audience, and penetrate the conversation going on in your target industry. You can become an insider who is trusted, not an outsider who is held at arm's length.

In today's economy, where consumers are in control and have access to more information than ever, one-size-fits-all businesses are struggling, and mass markets are fragmenting into widely dispersed niche markets. The same market forces are affecting lawyers and law firms. Most law firm clients aren't searching for a generalist lawyer who can address every legal issue at a bargain price. They're assembling teams consisting of smart, specialized lawyers from an array of firms, each of whom is good at one thing. Cost, while still important, does not drive the decision. Clients are seeking a result, not a bargain.

When it comes to establishing a niche, the idea is to try to become known as the best, or nearly the best, in a narrow market; like Scott Becker serving surgical centers in the greater Chicago area. Discard any illusion of building a big, broad practice (at least for now), and start figuring out how you can attract attention, build trust, and engender loyalty within a narrowly focused niche market. What you'll come to find is that serving a narrow market is often a precursor to serving a broader one.

Indeed, focusing on a niche does not equate to settling for mediocrity or putting a cap on your potential. Serving a "narrow" market is not the same as serving a "small" market. Most narrow markets are, in fact, quite large. A franchise lawyer who specializes only in serving fast-casual restaurants, or an IP litigator who only serves domestic semiconductor companies, are both focused on multi-billion dollar markets.

Some niche markets may start small, but then become very big. When Joe Flom was a young lawyer at Skadden, Arps, Slate, Meagher & Flom, it was conventional wisdom that white-shoe Wall Street law firms should avoid hostile corporate takeover work. There wasn't that much work in this space to begin with (at least relative to what was to come), and the work was considered unseemly.

Flom, who didn't fit the mold of the typical Wall Street lawyer, saw this as an opportunity. He dove into hostile takeover work during the 1960s, and when the corporate takeover boom of the 1970s and 1980s came around, he was positioned to be the go-to lawyer, and Skadden the go-to firm, in this space. Flom was so feared and respected in his niche that companies concerned with becoming takeover targets paid him hefty retainer fees so that he couldn't be engaged to lead a corporate raid against them. In essence, they bought expensive insurance to avoid facing Flom in battle. This tactic was known as "sterilizing Joe." He couldn't come after you if he worked for you. All of the law firms that considered this type of work undignified in the past were racing to catch up. Flom's focus on this niche didn't just benefit him; it lifted his colleagues and firm as well. Skadden's explosive growth, and expansion into new practice areas and markets in the 1970s, 1980s, and beyond, was in large part due to Flom's focus on a relatively small and "undesirable" niche market in the 1960s.

Three thousand miles away, at almost the same time that Flom was starting to make a splash on Wall Street, a recent law school graduate named Larry Sonsini joined a small group of lawyers who started a law firm in Palo Alto, California. The firm focused on serving young entrepreneurs and their venture capital-backed technology companies. Sonsini and his colleagues saw an opportunity that others did not, which was to build a full-scale law firm that catered to members of an emerging industry.

This strategy, focused on exclusively representing fledgling technology companies, may seem obvious now, but it was revolutionary in the early 1960s. And as we now know, it succeeded in a significant way. Wilson Sonsini Goodrich & Rosati is one of the premier law firms representing technology companies around the world. Its reputation stems from the vision and courage of lawyers like Larry Sonsini, who decades ago recognized an opportunity represent a small niche market that grew into a big one.

Carving out a niche is easier said than done. It requires courage and few embrace the challenge. Visualize a continuum on which "broad general practice" lies on one end, and "narrow niche practice" lies on the other. Most lawyers fall somewhere in the middle. They don't try to be all things to all clients, but they like to keep their options open. Just look at the laundry list of practice areas that most lawyers identify on their website bios. It's not possible to be an expert in so many different areas of the law, but lawyers present prospective clients with a buffet of options nonetheless. Each decision a lawyer makes to cast a wider net makes it less obvious to the marketplace what the lawyer does, or at least does well. The lawyer is generally relevant to many, but specifically relevant to few.

The tendency to cast a wide net is driven by a fear of missing out, and the misguided notion that if you provide more options, you'll have more opportunities as a result. It's also driven by the desire for variety, and the urge to do something different each day.

But there are consequences from fear and a downside to variety. The less focused you are, the more commoditized you become. The more commoditized you become, the more alternatives there are to what you offer. The more alternatives there are, the less pricing power you have. As we all learned in Econ 101, price elasticity results from the availability of substitutes in a market. The more alternatives that exist in a market, the lower the price will be, and vice versa.

By commoditizing yourself, you can insulate yourself from fears of missed opportunities, and indulge desires for variety, but this comes at a price. While there is comfort in being a generalist, it is false comfort. When you have a niche specialty, you may lose opportunities that don't align with it. But when you're a generalist, you're almost certain to miss out on the more beneficial opportunities that present themselves to narrowly focused legal experts.

> "Associates need to run their careers like a business and interact with clients, partners and colleagues as such. If they offer a commodity, that puts them in a place that makes them compete on price. They need to provide a service and work product that is tailored, unique, valuable, and sets them apart in some fashion."
>
> — RANDY JUIP, PARTNER AT FOLEY, BARON, METZGER & JUIP

The market for legal services is too competitive to have "some" expertise or "general" industry knowledge. To become a recognized expert in a particular field of practice, you must go all-in on a niche.

THE INTERSECTION OF INTERESTS, EXPERIENCE, AND MARKET OPPORTUNITIES

Going all-in requires making some hard choices. In rock climbing, the most difficult part of every climb is called the crux. It's the spot on the rock face at which most climbers fail. When it comes to your journey in building a personal brand, the crux is the point at which you have to choose a niche focus. Choosing something—a practice or industry focus—is not the hardest part. What is most difficult is accepting that by choosing your area of focus, you have to put everything else aside. I urge you to get past this crux. The climb gets much easier once you do.

For most lawyers, niche areas of expertise lie at the intersection of interests, experience, and market opportunities. If you can determine what you like to do, what you're good at, and where market opportunities exist, and then find some commonality among them, you'll be in good shape when it comes to carving out a niche.

Consider the experience of a former colleague of mine. Fairly early in his career, he established himself as a skilled corporate bankruptcy lawyer (what he was good at, but a broad, "big pond" area of the law). While his knowledge and experience was in U.S. bankruptcy law, he always had an interest in aspects of international law (what interested him). A career in U.S. bankruptcy law does not necessarily lend itself to exposure to international law issues, but that didn't stop him. He identified opportunities to develop expertise in the narrow but important area of how the U.S. Bankruptcy Code and U.K. pen-

sion law intersect and impact each other. He honed his expertise in
this area before the 2008 financial crisis and restructuring wave, and
when the wave hit (the market opportunity), he was well positioned
for a number of large, important engagements in U.S. bankruptcy
cases that involved these international issues.

In the next chapter, we're going to explore what it takes to generate awareness of your personal brand. Before you can generate brand
awareness, however, you need to decide *what you want people to be
aware of.* This requires narrowing the focus of your practice. A helpful place to start is determining what you like to do and then what
you're good at. If there's a market for the type of services you hope
to provide, no matter how narrow, or even small, it may seem now,
you're on your way to defining your niche.

As a young lawyer who may be struggling with your day-to-day
responsibilities, it may seem daunting and premature to start thinking about picking a practice niche. After all, the point at which you

will have clients of your own probably seems a long way off. Ignore the voice in your head that's telling you that this important priority can wait until later. It's never too early to start building your brand within a narrow niche. And by defining your niche, you'll then have a market in mind in which to compete. Your personal brand will be the currency you need to compete effectively.

Keep in mind, especially early in your career, that your niche may be something that you develop entirely within the confines of your firm. Skadden partner Brian McCarthy urges young associates to: "Become an expert in one thing that can be helpful to your team. You can build a lot of confidence with others by becoming an expert in the mechanics of what you are working on, such as figuring out when the filing deadline is, or the process of getting the right documents to the right people at the right time." You can level up and broaden your substantive knowledge of the law over time, but at these early stages of your career it is critical to build confidence with those inside your firm, and mastery of mechanics can be a beneficial way to achieve this objective.

Start small. Your niche will grow over time. But always remember that the goal of building a strong personal brand is not to become widely known. Awareness among people and within markets that don't align with your interests, expertise, and business development aspirations is of little benefit. The objective is to become widely known as a *recognized expert* within a *narrow domain*. As we just discussed, the first step in the process of building a personal brand is to choose a specific, narrow market in which to focus your brand-building efforts. The next step, which we'll now address, involves creating awareness of your personal brand within that narrow market.

Deal and Deposition—Narrow Your Practice or Industry Area of Specialization, But Build a Broad Set of Technical Skills

While sitting in a bankruptcy courtroom during my first year as a lawyer, I observed a partner in my firm cross-examine a witness. Another partner, a litigator who was sitting next to me in court, leaned over and whispered: "Watch closely and learn something." During a subsequent conversation, I learned that what others admired about the lawyer conducting the cross-examination was the depth and breadth of his skill set. He was as comfortable in a boardroom as he was in a courtroom. He could negotiate a deal as efficiently as he could conduct a deposition or cross-examination. The week before the court hearing, he had overseen an auction process involving hundreds of millions of dollars of corporate assets.

Large firms have experts in almost every conceivable skill set and practice area. If you're a bankruptcy lawyer, you can always tap a litigator to examine a witness. But you'll become a stronger and more well-rounded lawyer by getting out of your comfort zone and learning to do it yourself.

It's important for lawyers to develop *narrow domain expertise* in a practice or industry to build a powerful personal brand and a strong book of business, but having a *broad set of technical skills* can be an equally important asset. You want to go narrow and deep when it comes to the market in which you compete, but have a diverse set of tools (i.e., the ability to both take a deposition and negotiate a contract) to serve that market. At a minimum, young lawyers should strive to have first-hand familiarity with the processes involved in different aspects of the legal practice.

> **"A career is a long time, and practice areas and industries come and go. You need to be able to do a number of things."**
> — BILL MCKENNA, PARTNER AT FOLEY & LARDNER

This is true for many reasons. First, it can distinguish a young lawyer from their peers. Let's say that a last-minute deposition is required in a corporate restructuring matter. In a big firm, it's likely possible to find a litigator to step in, but you can bet that the young bankruptcy lawyer who raises their hand and steps up while their colleagues shrink away will gain respect. Second, it's an essential skill for business development. Lawyers don't only have opportunities to develop business in their primary areas of expertise. Transactional lawyers don't only come across potential clients in need of help with transactions and litigators don't just have opportunities with potential clients facing litigation. Having familiarity—being able to speak the language, spot issues, and understand the processes—with other areas of the law, and the skills associated with those areas is critical to cross-selling. Third, a lawyer with a broad skill set keeps doors open down the road. If a lawyer ever decides to practice in a smaller firm environment, they will find that they can't as easily pass off a deposition as they could at a big firm.

"In the early stages of your career, develop a broad skill set. You'll be a better lawyer for it. Pay attention to what is exciting to you in terms of a particular issue of law or industry. But things change way too quickly, and if an industry or legal area changes then you'll be left without a strong foundation to regroup and build upon. You need to be aware that a niche can disappear."
— FELICIA PERLMAN, PARTNER AT SKADDEN, ARPS, SLATE, MEAGHER & FLOM

Markets shift. Industries come and go. Practice areas get hot, then not. As Abbott Nicholson partner Bill Gilbride said, "If you're twenty-seven years old and you stay healthy and continue to practice, you could be in it for close to fifty years. Things change." Bill started his career doing real estate transactions and then the economy collapsed. He then had to adapt to become a commercial litigator.

Want to be the "five-tool" athlete among your associate class? Get out of your silo, and get into your discomfort zone once in awhile. Narrow the focus of the industry your serve, but broaden your technical skill set to guard against inevitable changes in market conditions. That way, if market conditions do change, you can bring your technical skills to bear in a different industry niche.

10

Essential Step Two: Create Awareness

"Life isn't about finding yourself. Life is about creating yourself."

– GEORGE BERNARD SHAW

The first step in building a powerful personal brand is choosing a narrow niche market to serve. The second step is understanding, and then deploying, the core strategies that create awareness of your personal brand. What follows is a discussion of these strategies. While these are not the only strategies you can pursue, they are "core" in the sense that they've worked well for generations of successful lawyers before you, and they'll work for you, too. There are more, including things like advertising, public relations, or starting a podcast, but I address ones that can realistically be implemented within the constraints of a modern-day law firm.

Some firms may not have a problem with an associate starting a podcast (if so, go for it!), but in most cases, there would be so much red tape involved that the headaches might outweigh the benefits.

These strategies are important at every stage of a lawyer's career. They are not "associate strategies." They are universal strategies that work regardless of experience level. But in the context of this book, I set out to describe how associates in approximately their first through fourth years of practice can employ them to best effect. For example, some of what I say about the issue of one-on-one networking may seem unimportant or irrelevant to lawyers with twenty years of experience and big books of business. That's okay: This book is for you, not them.

The four core strategies to build your personal brand are:

1. Intrapreneurship

2. One-on-One Networking

3. Public Speaking

4. Writing

Clients often ask me: "Of these four strategies, which one works best?" My answer: "All of them!"

They all work equally well *if you put the work in.* You can't expect results if you just dabble and try to squeeze this stuff in when you can. You need to block time on your calendar at least every week, and ideally every day, to engage in activities that generate awareness of your personal brand.

Take action. Experiment. Determine what is working and make adjustments. Author Jim Collins calls this approach "firing bullets before cannonballs." When considering a new strategy, fire off some bullets before unloading your cannon. This allows you to see if the bullets hit their mark, and then adjust your aim accordingly. Dial in your target, then load the cannons and unleash everything you've got. You need to try a little bit of everything—for example, content marketing, public speaking, social media—to determine what works and what you have an aptitude for. Then you can go all in on your strengths.

PRACTICE INTRAPRENEURSHIP

For many years, it was widely accepted that law schools failed to teach practice management and business development skills that are essential for lawyers to learn to become successful. Things have changed significantly in recent years. Law schools are implementing curriculum and programs that address the business issues law students will face when they become practicing lawyers. While this is a big step forward, and lawyers are coming out of school more prepared than ever before, the reality is that most aspects of business development cannot be taught in the classroom.

The skills attorneys must practice to develop a book of business must be acquired in the real world, through observation, trial, and error. Especially error. Yes, business development is mostly about failure, which is one of the main reasons that many lawyers, who are competitive and like to win, don't relish the business development process.

If you talk to any successful professional who consistently engages in business development activity, they will tell you that they lose the sale far more often than they win it. But there's a bright side to losing. With every failure comes the chance to learn and adapt. Experienced attorneys are not discouraged by unsuccessful efforts. They see each "failure" as an opportunity to get better and draw lessons from the experience that help guide their future actions. This mindset shift, which requires a "growth mindset," leads to more business development activity, not less, and ultimately more success.

For young, relatively inexperienced attorneys at law firms with high billing rates and sophisticated corporate clients, the challenge is that most are not in a position to be pitching their services. They haven't yet developed the skill set, judgment, and management skills necessary to develop business at this level. Spending much, if any, precious time chasing work during one's first few years of practice is a misallocation of resources.

You will have to develop business at some point to advance and make partner, but you don't want to spin your wheels chasing business you will never catch. At this point in your career, you're just getting comfortable playing a supporting role to other attorneys, and you are not ready to be the headliner just yet. Learn to do the little things well before worrying about the big things. It's often the little things that make the biggest difference.

Brian McCarthy is the managing partner of the Los Angeles office of Skadden, Arps, Slate, Meagher & Flom. Early in his career he worked on a deal with a difficult partner. Rather than accepting the challenging nature of the working relationship, Brian set out to improve it. An opportunity for improvement arose when the partner went out of town and Brian took it upon himself to read all of the major newspapers and clip out (yes, pre-Internet days) every news story that he could find that mentioned the partner's clients. He assembled the news stories in a binder and had them waiting for the partner upon his return so that when he came back to the office he was thoroughly up to speed. By taking the initiative, the partner's perception of Brian and the dynamic of their working relationship changed dramatically.

Instead of focusing on solving the problems of someone outside of the firm, Brian looked for an opportunity to serve someone within the firm, which allowed him to impress an influential partner in the firm. This story highlights an important principle of personal brand building for young lawyers: While most experienced attorneys should engage in lots of entrepreneurship with a focus on developing relationships outside of the firm, junior attorneys should actively engage in entrepreneurship with their colleagues inside the firm. Brian McCarthy's experience assembling news clippings that mentioned a partner's clients is an excellent example of this type of internal entrepreneurship. It's called "intrapreneurship."

Intrapreneurship in this context is a focus on brand building activities within a law firm. It means building your reputation among colleagues through internally-focused initiatives. It's engaging in activities that allow you to hone the skills and characteristics, such as strong writing and presentation skills, good judgment, and confidence, that you will need when it's time to compete for work in the business world. Brian McCarthy urges young lawyers to, "Practice skill and reputation building by working internally within the system. As you develop a reputation for excellent work, you'll start getting calls because word gets around."

Accordingly, if partnership is your objective, your intrapreneurial activities will give your colleagues—who are often geographically dispersed—more to know you by than impersonal metrics such as hours billed and fees generated. They'll be more likely to want to staff you on their engagements, include you when it comes time to pitch client work, and be aware of your strengths when called upon to make decisions related to your advancement within the firm.

Focusing on intrapreneurship reflects an understanding of how business gets generated by most lawyers at law firms. Obviously, business comes from relationships with potential clients and referral sources outside of the firm. But lawyers can also generate a great deal of business from colleagues within their firms.

For example, lawyers will leave your firm to go to another one and become referral sources. Others will go in-house and be in a position to send you business directly. Build a strong reputation among your colleagues and someday you may work for them in an attorney/client engagement. Impress lots of people internally, and you'll be well-positioned to inherit clients from other lawyers when they retire, move in-house, or otherwise transition out of the firm. The more people you reach through your intrapreneurial activities, the stronger your brand will be and the more success you'll have.

There are countless ways to practice intrapreneurship and build your personal brand within your law firm. Here are a few ideas.

- Most firms have associate committees. Get involved.
- Pro bono opportunities are prevalent, and pro bono success stories get celebrated within most firms. Take on a matter and do an excellent job.
- Firms publish numerous newsletters and blogs but often lack writing and editing resources to keep up with demands for content. Write great content yourself. Better yet, co-author an article with a partner and take charge of the process.
- Many firms utilize outdated or inefficient processes or procedures when it comes to things like project management and internal and external communication. Come up with an innovative alternative.
- Most associates hunker down in their offices, waiting for opportunities to find them. Seek them out instead by walking the halls and interacting with partners. Find out who is pitching for work and offer to help out.
- There are countless training and educational opportunities for associates at most firms. Learn and grow.

- All firms have rainmakers who have business development figured out. Network with them, observe them, and mimic their habits and behaviors.

- Like Brian McCarthy, look for opportunities to keep colleagues informed about a client or an industry. Become a valuable resource.

You may not be seasoned enough to generate business from a Fortune 500 company at this point in your career, but there are plenty of opportunities to be an intrapreneur and add value within your firm. Get active and involved. This will serve you well when you're ready to start developing your own book of business.

NETWORKING STRATEGIES

Let's start with something obvious: To build a network, you must engage in networking. We will address the best ways to cultivate, nurture, and grow relationships with existing members of your network in chapters to come. This is called "warm" networking. The purpose of this chapter is to discuss "cold" networking, which involves making contact and establishing relationships with people who are not currently in your network.

Cold networking takes place in many settings, from industry events to the sidelines of your child's soccer game. The objective of cold networking is to put your best foot forward when interacting with new people so you can get to know them on a personal level. In almost all interactions, you will need to convey that you're a good person before you will get the opportunity to demonstrate that you're a good lawyer. Prospective clients have many alternatives available to them, so among those alternatives they typically hire the person they like to spend time with.

The tips that follow will help you to make a strong first impression on people you meet while networking, which is the first step toward building relationships that result in new business.

Cold Networking Tip 1: Do Your Research

You may be going into a situation that requires cold networking, but that doesn't mean you have to go into it completely cold. There are lots of ways that you can lay the groundwork necessary to make interactions at networking events go more smoothly and successfully.

There are ways to determine in advance who will be attending an event. If your firm sponsors or purchases a table at an event, you can often get your hands on the attendee list before the event. Even if you can't secure the attendee list, you can still get a pretty good sense of who will be there by identifying event speakers, other businesses who are sponsoring the event (you can be sure that at least some people who work there will be attending), and people who serve on the board and committees of the event organizer. Many events will create an associated hashtag that people will use when posting on social media, and the appearance of the hashtag on Twitter or LinkedIn can serve as a digital clue as to who will be in attendance.

Conducting research will allow you to identify people at the event who you'd like to meet, and to conduct "human intel" that aids in introductory conversations. By knowing what school someone attended, what their professional focus is, and what they're passionate about, you can guide conversations toward their areas of interest. People like to talk about things that matter to them. With the limited time you have during a conversation to make a good first impression, the faster you can put someone at ease by asking questions within their comfort zone the better.

By doing your research, you can make contact with other attendees in advance of an event in a meaningful way. Identify a few people you'd like to meet and send them notes a week before the event expressing your desire to grab a cup of coffee or cocktail during the event. Don't ask for the opportunity to "pick someone's brain." This comes across as lazy and self-centered. If you can figure out what matters to them, then you can suggest a meeting that addresses their interests and not your own.

Never walk into a room cold. Take the time to warm things up in advance.

Cold Networking Tip 2: Expect the Unexpected

Chris Sacca is a lawyer and legendary venture capitalist (now retired from investing in his early 40s) who was one of the first investors in companies like Twitter, Uber, and Stripe. He worked as an associate at Fenwick & West before he was let go during the dot-com bust. During a podcast interview, Sacca discussed his approach to searching for up-and-coming start-up companies to invest in. According to Sacca, the key is getting out there, meeting interesting people, and discarding biases about what types of people are worth investing time in.

Sacca told a story about at an event he attended in California. The day's speeches were followed by a dinner at which attendees had the opportunity to sit with their favorite speakers. Seats were taken on a first-come-first-served basis and Sacca arrived a bit late so all of the tables he wanted to sit at were full. In the back of the room he noticed a table occupied by a single person, a speaker Sacca did not know named Shivaji Siroya.

He grabbed a seat next to Siroya and struck up a conversation. Sacca spent the next two hours entranced. Siroya was the founder and CEO of a startup called Tala, which helps customers in emerging economies borrow money and develop credit scores. Sacca made an investment in Tala and served on its board (something he rarely does). He described Tala as the "most exciting company" in his portfolio.

The moral of Sacca's story: While networking, expect the unexpected. You never know where business will come from, so be open to new relationships with people who don't fit the mold of a prototypical potential client or referral source.

Everyone is in the same boat at networking events. Few relish the idea of walking up to someone they don't know and introducing themselves. Take the initiative to meet new people. Don't huddle around someone holding court and don't remain in the comfort zone of your colleagues. Take a cue from Chris Sacca's experience and work the edges of the room. You never know what you'll find.

Cold Networking Tip 3: Put Your Phone Away

Networking is all about dancing with discomfort. It's never easy to strike up conversations with people you don't know. In stressful moments like this, it's easy to fall back on coping mechanisms.

Smartphones are like security blankets for many of us; whenever we're uncomfortable or bored, we pull them out and start scrolling because it's a way to numb or distract from the discomfort. However, not only does the presence of your phone prevent you from engaging with others, but it stops other from approaching you as well. No one is going to walk up and introduce themselves if your face is buried in your phone.

A phone is networking kryptonite—leave it in the car, or at least muted in your pocket, and keep it there.

Cold Networking Tip 4: Show Interest in Others

I've been happily married for seventeen years, so it's been awhile since I've been on a first date. But what I remember about the first-date experience is that there was a much higher likelihood of a second one if I talked less and listened more. Networking is like dating.

Instead of being ready to talk about yourself, go into networking events enthusiastic to listen to and learn from others. Accomplished networkers (and those who are successful at business development) are active listeners. Train yourself to approach encounters with new people with curiosity and genuine interest. Do research to arm yourself with questions to elicit information about other people.

Talking about yourself may avoid awkward gaps in conversations, but asking questions and listening intently to someone else is what builds rapport and results in meaningful relationships.

Cold Networking Tip 5: Ditch the Elevator Speech

Few people like delivering an elevator speech. Almost no one likes listening to someone else's elevator speech. So why do we feel compelled to have one? The perceived need derives from a belief that we need to be ready to talk about ourselves in networking settings. But since no one seems to want to hear an elevator speech, which typically comes across as rehearsed and self-indulgent, it's best to ditch yours.

That said, you still need to be prepared to succinctly and confidently answer the following question, which is asked of almost everyone at some point during a networking event: "So what do you do for a living?"

My suggestion is to craft an answer that is brief, results-oriented, and invites further inquiry. Contrast this with the typical lawyer's elevator speech, which tends to be a wordy recitation of employment history and a laundry list of practice area experience.

Here's my example of a brief, results-oriented introduction that almost always leads to further inquiry: "I help lawyers build powerful personal brands and profitable books of business."

I don't go into exhaustive detail about what I do. Instead I keep it short and focus only on what results I deliver for clients. Assuming I'm networking among members of my target market (lawyers and legal marketing professionals), this client-focused introduction often leads to lots of questions about the means by which I help lawyers achieve such results. I get to talk about myself and my work at the invitation of others—not because I forced the issue.

Cold Networking Tip 6: Find Networking Whitespace

You're busy and your capacity to network is limited, so choose where to spend your limited time wisely. It's possible that the best use of your time is at bar association events with other lawyers. After all, other lawyers can be excellent referral sources. But it's important to think more broadly. You don't want to be dependent on other professionals to supply your pipeline of work. Take into account your niche focus and find events where members of your target audience gather. If your niche is narrow, you may discover that you're one of the only attorneys in attendance. There are events that attract many lawyers. You should consider attending these events, too. But there's networking whitespace out there for you to take advantage of if you look hard enough for it.

Final (and Most Important) Cold Networking Tip: Follow Up

The most critical cold networking advice of all: Follow up with people you meet; and, no, this doesn't just mean adding them to your network on LinkedIn. Follow up with an email, phone call, or a handwritten note a few days after the event. Better yet, try to set up lunch or drinks to continue the conversation.

If you want to leave a lasting impression, you need to find ways to stand out among the dozens of other lawyers that a high-value prospect will likely meet at an event. By following up thoughtfully, and finding ways to sustain the conversation over time, you will distinguish yourself.

PUBLIC SPEAKING STRATEGIES

Many lawyers are terrified at the idea of public speaking. If the idea of public speaking induces anxiety in you, take comfort in knowing you're not alone. Jerry Seinfeld tells a joke about a study that found that most people fear public speaking more than they do death. According to Seinfeld, this means the average person at a funeral would rather be in the casket than giving the eulogy.

Here's the good news: You can get better and become more comfortable with public speaking if you practice. Warren Buffett is widely renowned as a brilliant public speaker, but that was not always the case. At the age of twenty-one, Buffett started his career as a stockbroker. He was scared to speak in public. Knowing that this fear would hold him back throughout his career, he enrolled in a Dale Carnegie course on public speaking. Since then he has practiced his craft and has become one of the best communicators in the business. Buffett believes that failing to put the work in to become an effective communicator is akin to giving up on your potential.

While it's comforting to know that fear of public speaking is common, it's essential to overcome this fear because there will come a point in your career when you have to do it. It's better to practice it now than to be paralyzed by it later.

Fear of public speaking holds us back from our professional ambitions. It prevents us from contributing to meetings despite having good ideas to share. It keeps us from networking successfully. It leads us to pass on opportunities to share our expertise with a broader audience. It inhibits us from advocating effectively on behalf of our clients. It stops us from assuming leadership positions that require some form of public speaking. As Warren Buffett realized as a young man, it hampers our careers.

On the other hand, those who overcome their fears and embrace the power of public speaking can build strong awareness of their personal brands. They use public speaking to become known as a recognized expert, and then leverage their expert status into business development opportunities.

For Skadden, Arps, Slate, Meagher & Flom partner Brian Mc-Carthy, public speaking has long been a significant component of his personal brand building and business development repertoire. He began public speaking almost by happenstance. Early in his career, Brian was asked by a conference organizer to step in at the last minute for another speaker who was unable to present. The conference was geared toward members of the corporate niche that Brian focused on, so he jumped at the opportunity and delivered a compelling presentation.

From this opportunity additional ones presented themselves. Brian has been refining his keynote presentation ever since, delivering it to bigger and more influential audiences over time. Depending on the interests of a particular audience, he's able to adapt and expand upon discrete parts of his presentation. Public speaking has helped him to form new relationships that have led to significant new business opportunities.

Public speaking helps to establish authority and increase name recognition in your field. It provides opportunities to rub shoulders with other thought leaders. It gets people in your network talking about you and your ideas. It generates interest in your personal brand.

Every young lawyer should develop a keynote speech. It should be a sixty-minute presentation (that can be edited down to thirty minutes, as necessary) that covers a topic of interest to members of a niche audience. The objective of a strong keynote is to establish your authority as a subject matter expert. Pick an issue that is trending in your niche industry and go deep on it. Do the research, talk to other leaders, synthesize the best ideas and stories, and weave them together in a compelling narrative.

The great thing about content development for public speaking is that you only need one speech and slide deck to be effective and create awareness of your personal brand. Because your speech content is delivered live to an audience, you can give the same speech over and over to different groups, and while it's a fresh experience every time for your audience, it's old hat to you. On the other hand, if you publish written content, you need to come up with something new every time you sit down at the keyboard. Written content is an important personal branding tool, but it's best supplemented with public speaking. Writing generates ideas for speaking and vice versa.

Once you develop your keynote, you can seek out opportunities to deliver it to your niche audience. You'll likely start small at venues such as local chambers of commerce and client "lunch and learn" meetings, but that's okay—even advisable. Over time, as you hone your skills and your content, you'll get the chance to present before larger audiences. Awareness of your brand will grow larger as a result.

Are you ready to step up to the microphone? Here are some tips on how you can become a better public speaker.

Public Speaking Tip 1: Practice

Public speaking is like exercise. You'll only get better if you work the muscle. John Tredennick, CEO of Catalyst Systems Repository and a former litigator at Holland & Hart, discussed how he became a better speaker in an article for Attorney at Work. It came down to practice. "In my second year at Holland & Hart, I realized that I knew nothing about speaking, and it hit me that if I was ever going to succeed, I needed to speak, and speak well," John said. "I was terrible when I first started, but I put the time in regardless, and gradually I got good at it. I'm not a nervous speaker because I'm prepared. I work hard at it, and that fills me with energy."

Practice in public. Present to your colleagues about a specific topic you recently researched. Start a "brown bag" lunch series for a client, or for members of an organization that you belong to. Find a group of colleagues who are also interested in developing their public speaking chops, and provide feedback to one another. It's easy to assume that only those who were born with the "gift of the gab" make good public speakers, but those for whom public speaking comes naturally often plateau because they don't practice enough. Public speaking is a craft, and like any craft, those who become skilled craftsmen put the most work into it.

Public Speaking Tip 2: Recruit a Team

Public speaking can be scary when you're on stage all by yourself. If you forget a line or experience a technical malfunction, you're on your own to work through the challenges. A way to combat this problem is to find a partner or a team to help you ease into public speaking. There's no rule that a speech has to be delivered by a single individual, so recruit someone else in your firm to help address a topic, or form a panel and find a moderator to present as a team. It's far easier for most people to riff off of the ideas and insights of others than it is to have the sole responsibility for captivating an audience for sixty minutes.

Public Speaking Tip 3: Create a Structure

Crafting a great speech is no different than creating any other piece of work product meant to engage and persuade an audience in that it requires a clear structure. Creating a well-structured speech helps you remember what to say and allows the audience to understand you.

There are many different types of speech structures that you can use. There's "numerical" structure in which you address a set of challenges and best practices to overcome them. There's "chronological" structure in which you describe a step-by-step process. There are "problem and solution" and "compare and contrast" structures in which you bounce back and forth between issues. There are all kinds of different speech structures you can use. The structure does not matter. You just need to have one.

Public Speaking Tip 4: Deliver a Performance

There's nothing worse than listening to someone read a speech. Well, actually, there is something worse, which is listening to someone try to regurgitate a speech they memorized word-for-word. It always comes across as stilted, uninteresting, and unpersuasive.

This is why it's important to develop a single keynote and then deliver it over and over. When you know your material so well that you don't even have to think about it, you can deliver a performance and not simply a speech. You can be spontaneous and take cues from the audience rather than being stuck inside your head the whole time. You can focus on movement and gestures instead of searching for what you're going to say next. Performers rehearse like crazy and when they get on stage they appear instinctual and effortless. These are the nuances that separate performers from mere speakers.

Public Speaking Tip 5: Prepare for the Worst

Something will go wrong during almost every speech you give. Your slide deck won't work. There will be a problem with audio. Someone's phone will ring. The fire alarm will go off. You'll forget your content. Things you never anticipated will go awry. Prepare for these eventualities.

I learned this lesson the hard way. I was presenting to a group of legal marketers about the topic of content marketing and began my talk with a quip about how content marketing is making traditional advertising increasingly irrelevant. What I didn't realize, but should have by doing my homework in advance, was that one of the primary sponsors of the event was the largest business trade publication in town.

The publication was, of course, sponsoring the event in hopes of generating advertising opportunities from the marketing professionals in attendance. The sponsor representative got up from her seat and left the room after I suggested that advertising was losing relevance and effectiveness. Awkward, yes, but I recovered (although not for long). Five minutes later the projector displaying my slides fizzled out and there was no back-up. I've learned since that if this happens you just need to plow through the presentation with no visuals. At the time, which was early in my public speaking career, I spent several minutes monkeying around with the technology with no luck. I completely lost the audience.

When giving a speech, if something can go wrong it probably will. You need to anticipate things in advance and be ready to overcome them. An amateur gets derailed by such things. A professional rises above them. Be prepared.

Public speaking is a critical skill for young lawyers to learn. Throughout your career, you'll be expected to perform and deliver persuasive content in many different contexts, and from the courtroom to the boardroom, to your firm's conference room among your colleagues, you need to be ready to make an impact. Approach these opportunities not as something to be feared, but rather as a way to build your reputation as a persuasive and articulate expert.

WRITING STRATEGIES

Implicit in everything addressed in this book is the principle that consumers of legal services desire expertise above all else. Unless and until expertise can be conveyed and validated through referral or reputation, one of the best and only ways that it can be demonstrated is through written thought leadership expressed in the marketplace of ideas. In modern marketing parlance this is known as "content marketing." Generating and disseminating compelling content builds trust and awareness, and positions the content creator as an expert. It's another long-game tactic with a focus on relationship building not the hard sell. But while it's not the hard sell, content marketing is selling in the sense that it attracts people to you.

Written content is like gravity. It keeps people, companies, and organizations in your orbit. Those who become aware of you stay aware of you as a result of your content. Those not in your orbit move into it after becoming exposed to your content. Sharing content is also a respectful and thoughtful way to remain engaged with clients and keep them in your orbit during gaps between engagements.

When someone who is in your orbit experiences a problem or has an opportunity related to a topic that you previously wrote about, you'll be high on that person's list as a lawyer who possesses the requisite experience and expertise to help overcome the problem or seize the opportunity, as the case may be. While your reader may not be ready to act immediately, additional thought leadership will keep you on their radar screen, and when the time is right the relationship will shift from one of reader and writer to that of client and attorney.

Generate and share content. Keep contacts in your orbit. When an opportunity arises, you'll be top of mind. Sounds simple, right? In some ways it is but it takes a long-term commitment. Expect results from your writing—just don't expect them immediately. As you'll learn through the following examples, attorneys who invest time to produce valuable content generate lots of value in return.

Writing a Blog to Build a Personal Brand: Mark Herrmann

Mark Herrmann is Vice President and Deputy General Counsel at insurance giant AON Corporation, author of *The Curmudgeon's Guide to Practicing Law*, and previously was a partner at Jones Day. While at Jones Day he was faced with the challenge of trying to establish a drug and device product liability practice from scratch.

To build awareness for the practice, Mark started writing articles for drug and device industry publications. In 2006, he began the Drug and Device Law Blog with a co-blogger from another firm. While lawyer blogs seem ubiquitous now (some even consider them antiquated), at the time Mark was venturing into a relatively uncharted territory.

"At first we were writing for ourselves," Mark said. But they kept at it, publishing a post a day. After three years, the blog was getting 30,000 to 40,000 page views per month. Mark's content marketing led to significant business for the firm's new practice and established him as a thought leader in the field.

Mark engaged in other awareness-building activities, such as public speaking, but he buttressed everything with his written thought leadership. New opportunities arose from his efforts, including writing a book about drug and device cases for Oxford University Press. Within a relatively short period, he helped to grow the firm's new initiative into an eight-figure practice.

Writing a Book to Build a Personal Brand: John Trentacosta

One of the challenges lawyers face when pitching new business is adequately explaining to prospective clients why they are any better situated to help solve a specific problem than the multitude of other smart, hardworking lawyers competing in the marketplace. There are few better answers to the question "Why should I hire you to deal with this issue?" than "I wrote the book on it."

Nothing conveys expert status more completely and more quickly than writing a book. John Trentacosta, a partner at Foley & Lardner and one of the country's top automotive industry litigators, learned this lesson early in his career.

As a young lawyer, John began working in the automotive indus-

try as the modern-day tiered supply chain came into existence. At that time, companies started focusing more intently on their contracting practices, including the terms and conditions included in purchase and supply contracts, and how those terms interacted with the dictates of the Uniform Commercial Code. Not only was this John's area of practice, but he was genuinely interested in the legal issues associated with the automotive supply chain.

It occurred to John that it was very inefficient not to have a single source that addressed the contract case law concerning the manufacturing industry. Being an enterprising lawyer, John decided to take up the challenge himself.

After doing a bit of digging, he learned that other states had similar treatises, and he approached the Institute of Continuing Legal Education (a Michigan provider of legal education and resources) about creating something similar in Michigan. John's book, *Michigan Contract Law*, was published in 1998. A second edition was published in 2013. John is also co-author and general editor of *Michigan*

Legal Forms-Uniform Commercial Code, and he has written numerous articles related to Uniform Commercial Code and commercial litigation issues in various legal and other trade publications over the years.

According to John, being a published author on an issue of significance is "a great calling card" into the world of in-house counsel because it establishes instant credibility. Being published also leads to other opportunities. After publishing his first book, John experienced a meaningful upturn in the number and quality of opportunities to write and speak, further exposing him to his target market and building his reputation. Writing a book has a multiplier effect when it comes to building your brand.

Writing a Blog (and a Book) to Build a Personal Brand: Keith Lee

Keith Lee is an Alabama lawyer who has gained national prominence as a result of his blog and a book he authored. He's the brains behind Associate's Mind, which consistently ranks among the American Bar Association's list of top legal blogs to follow.

Keith started Associate's Mind as a third-year law student and kept it up when he began practicing. Within a few months of starting his career, Associate's Mind took off and became widely read. This attracted the attention of the American Bar Association, which approached Keith about writing a book. In 2013, only three years after he graduated from law school, Keith's book, *The Marble and the Sculptor*, was published.

Keith attributes much of his success as a lawyer to the time he has invested in his writing. While some argue that the heyday of blogging has passed, Keith believes that we're still in the early stages of this revolution in how lawyers create awareness and build brands. "Never before has it been easier to reach more people, more easily," Keith said. "It's not too late. We're still in the Wild West. Be interesting. Interesting will never go out of style."

According to Keith, the difference between a lawyer who is successful with a writing strategy and one who isn't is their level of commitment. He draws an analogy to fishing. "When fishing, you don't throw one cast and then quit if you don't catch anything," Keith said. "The same goes for writing. You need to stick with it."

One of the biggest lessons to take away from Mark, John, and Keith's experience with content marketing is that you get out what you put in. There's too much noise in the marketplace to expect anyone to read your writing unless it's interesting, unique, and valuable. You can't mail it in. You can't do what everyone else is doing. Many people are writing content. To stand out, share wisdom.

Instead of thinking about your writing as content marketing, approach it as "wisdom marketing." Imparting wisdom through your writing requires you to dig deeper. It requires a greater degree of education, substance, and thoughtfulness. It places a premium on quality. Only those who impart wisdom through their content can build a foundation of trust, loyalty, and mutual respect with their audience.

If you expect readers to give you their attention you must first give them your wisdom. Shallow thoughts are like mindless small talk in that they're easy to ignore. To form relationships with readers you must blaze new ground and inspire people on a deeper level. If you can do this, you will be at the leading edge of wisdom marketing.

Writing Tip 1: Six Ideas to Get You Started

There's no secret formula for producing great content. You just have to commit to a process and stick to it. The reason that many lawyers don't consistently write compelling content is probably the same reason people don't exercise every morning. Writing is hard and requires lots of discipline. Content production is also a non-billable task that is easy to defer until later. Here are six tips to get you started.

1. Shut down the distractions. Disable email notifications, close Internet browsers, and shut your door. Sit in the chair, put your fingers on the keyboard, and prioritize your writing time.

2. Just let it rip. Don't try to edit as you go. Get words on the page, sleep on it, and edit the next day.

3. Set a low bar. If you sit down with the intention of writing 1,000 polished words in two hours, odds are you'll walk away from most writing sessions feeling like a failure. Instead, shoot for two crappy pages. Set an easy-to-achieve goal that you'll frequently exceed, which will keep you coming back for more.

4. Take notes. Write about issues that arise during your workday. Many people agonize over writing topics and blame "writer's block" for their lack of production. To generate writing ideas be more mindful throughout the day and take notes as you go. Every interaction you have, every matter you work on, and every article you read contain nuggets of wisdom.

5. Get it out there. Don't be afraid to compete in the marketplace of ideas. You're smart and have a point of view, so share it. Use the publishing resources your firm makes available. Publish on LinkedIn or Medium. Find a trade publication in need of content. There is huge demand among publishers for good content; it just takes a little effort to find the right fit to reach your audience.

6. Stick with it for at least thirty days. It's easy to be habitual for a week. It's more challenging to plow forward for two or three weeks. Once you can get over that hump it gets easier. Hang in there and achieve some success (you will). Content creation will soon become an inviolable part of your routine.

Writing Tip 2: How Often and How Much You Should Write

Smart, savvy, and skilled lawyers can crank out lots of excellent content. The challenge is harnessing these resources to create a sustained, interesting, and effective content marketing initiative over time. Client work, new business pitches, and administrative work often get in the way of content creation and that blog post you need to write languishes at the bottom of your to-do list.

It's common for lawyers to quit creating content because their efforts don't generate a tangible return on investment quickly enough. While returns from good content can be significant, they almost never come immediately. Remember, like almost any awareness generating activity that you will engage in, with content creation you're playing the long game, and it's a game that requires both quantity and quality. You don't have to be as prolific as Judge Posner, but you do have to be consistent.

If you're maintaining a blog, try to write at least one post per month and preferably two. One should be original content. The other can aggregate links to news items and articles from third-party websites that cover topics of interest to your audience. Generally speaking, blog posts should be limited to 1,000 words or less.

Try to produce one longer piece per quarter for a trade journal or other outside publications. Every publication has its own guidelines, but if it's a substantive piece then expect to write between 1,000 and 2,000 words.

While there are certain conventions and guidelines that you will need to follow when implementing a writing strategy, don't obsess about form over substance. There is a lot of talk in marketing circles these days suggesting that all forms of content should be brief to accommodate readers' increasingly short attention spans. People don't have short attention spans—it's just that they don't have the time or patience for content that isn't interesting and valuable regardless of its length. If you can get your point across in 1,000 words or less then do so. But don't put yourself in a box if you have 3,000 valuable words to share.

Writing Tip 3: Where to Publish Your Content

Unless your firm provides you with a platform (such as a newsletter or quarterly publication), you will need to find a place to publish your content. Fortunately, many websites and trade publications are eager to publish thoughtful articles.

In fact, publishing on outside platforms is often preferable to publishing on those within your firm's domain. One of the challenges you'll face as a young lawyer getting started with a content marketing initiative is breaking through to the audiences you're hoping to reach. Until you've established that you're someone worth reading or listening to, you'll lack a certain amount of credibility with your audience.

A great way to build credibility is to leverage "social proof" through association with influencers who already have credibility with those you're trying to reach. Social proof is a term from psychology that refers to someone's level of perceived credibility. Are you attached to people, brands, or institutions that others already perceive as excellent? If so, that affiliation encourages others to view you as someone of high quality, too.

In the context of content marketing, this means that if your writing appears in a well-respected outside publication, as opposed to an internal publication that has low barriers to entry, people are likely to view you as "pre-vetted" and will be predisposed to listen to you. By publishing on the outside "influencer" platform, a lawyer who may have had trouble breaking through to an audience on their own is now perceived as more trustworthy and credible by prospects because the influencer platform that published the lawyer's work has already deemed their insights worthy of attention. By doing an end run around the metaphorical brick wall that many people erect as a defense mechanism against the flood of mediocre content floating around the marketplace of ideas, the lawyer's content can reach its intended target.

Writing Tip 4: How to Promote Your Content on LinkedIn

If you've done the hard work necessary to pick a niche, and started producing content that's relevant to members of your niche audience, then it's essential to get the content in front of that audience to create awareness of your thought leadership in the space.

Many lawyers make the mistake of assuming that their law firm marketing department will promote their content for them. Even if you're writing for your firm's blog, and the content is shared in an email newsletter, you need to have your own social media channel to share the content directly with members of your audience.

The platform you choose depends on a few factors, the most important of which is determining where members of your niche target market hang out online. For example, if you hope to build brand awareness among entrepreneurial members of a creative community, such as photographers or graphic artists, then Instagram might be the best social platform to make connections and share content. If you have a consumer-oriented niche, such as estate planning for young families who have recently had their first child, then Facebook may be your best bet.

If the focus of your practice is more corporate-oriented, then LinkedIn is an increasingly important place to make connections, share content, and build your brand. At the time this book was published, LinkedIn was approaching 600 million members worldwide. In recent years, LinkedIn has made improvements to make content sharing easier and more effective. LinkedIn is a professional network, which means that people are spending time there to do business.

LinkedIn has everything a young lawyer needs to establish relationships online that lead to new business offline. It's just a matter of leveraging the tools to best effect.

Here are a few steps to get your content in front of the right people on LinkedIn:

1. Craft Your Profile. The point of sharing content on LinkedIn is to create awareness of your brand and to position you as a thought leader and expert within your niche. The content you share on LinkedIn should draw people back to your LinkedIn profile. Create a profile that focuses on how you help your targeted audience of potential clients and referral sources achieve their goals and solve their problems. Your profile should make it clear who you are, what you do, and the unique value you can provide to members of your market niche.

2. Build Your Network. Once you've optimized your profile, find members of your target audience and invite them to connect. LinkedIn is a big, powerful search engine for finding your ideal audience. Use LinkedIn's search function to find people and filter results by factors including job title, geographic location, industry type, company name, and school. If you're clear on who you serve, then finding people with whom to connect using LinkedIn's tools is simple.

3. Join Groups. Beyond making personal connections, find LinkedIn groups that are relevant to your niche and join them. There are thousands of groups that focus on almost every industry niche imaginable. They consist of people with shared interests. Share content with members of the groups you belong to.

4. Share Content Published Elsewhere. There are several ways to share your content with your LinkedIn network. If you publish content on another platform, such as your firm's blog or a third-party website, then write a summary and share the article URL using the "LinkedIn Status Update" in your feed. If someone from your network "likes" your update, then it will be shared with their network. The more likes, comments, and shares you earn, the more broadly your content will be spread.

5. Publish Directly on LinkedIn. In addition to sharing content you publish elsewhere through status updates, you can publish content directly on LinkedIn's publishing platform. All LinkedIn members have access to the platform, so it provides an opportunity to expand your reach beyond your immediate network.

6. Share Other People's Valuable Content. Keep in mind that you shouldn't only be sharing your original content on LinkedIn. Add value to your network, and develop relationships with influencers within your niche, by sharing other people's content as well.

To learn more about the essential steps necessary to build a network, brand, and book of business using LinkedIn, download my free guide: "How to Make an Impact on LinkedIn: A Step-by-Step Guide for Lawyers." It's available at www.hcommunications.biz/books.

Writing Tip 5: Use Social Media Purposefully and Intentionally

Use social networks as much as necessary to promote your content, but as little as possible. Make sure the time you do spend on social networks is purposeful and intentional. Get in and get out.

This means resisting the urge to check social media at the first sign of boredom or as a means of procrastinating while gearing up to tackle a challenging task. Use social media only during short, predetermined blocks of time on your calendar. Don't use it as a form of escapism loosely disguised as business development or networking. Producing great work doesn't happen by scrolling through other people's status updates, pretty pictures, and pithy quotes.

Social media activity should also be very strategic. As a lawyer, your time is too valuable to proceed otherwise. Social media platforms are the same as every other form of media (TV, radio, print) in the sense that they are engineered to deliver content. The one big difference is that social media platforms rely on user-generated content.

This presents a strategic opportunity for smart lawyers who act like publishers or broadcasters on social media as opposed to consumers (i.e., a reader, listener or viewer). While at work, treat time spent on social media as a job and not a form of entertainment. Be a publisher of content not a consumer of it. Produce content so good that people can't ignore it.

Create valuable content. Publish it and then promote it on social media. Automate and systematize the process of distributing your content as much as possible. Get on, do what needs to be done, then get off and back to your important work. Leave the consumption to others.

Writing Tip 6: Regardless of its Form, Just Produce Great Content

While writing is a core element of a robust content marketing strategy, it's not the only way to attract and build an audience. Lawyers are creatively using video, podcasts, information graphics, Slide-Share decks, and many other content formats to get their messages out. There is no shortage of outlets for good content.

The lessons in this section are geared toward written content marketing but are broadly applicable to any content format you choose to use. Regardless of its form, the important thing is to get thoughtful and valuable content in front of your target market to stay top of mind and build your reputation as a thought leader worth listening to.

11

Essential Step Three: Cultivate and Grow Your Network

"No one is useless in this world who lightens the burdens of another."

– CHARLES DICKENS

Shifts in markets, luck, timing, serendipity, and many other external influences will impact your ability to develop business. However, the most important determinant of business development success, which is the strength of your network, is within your control.

The objective of brand awareness is not to gain broad fame and notoriety; it's to build a strategic network within your practice niche that enables and empowers you to develop business. Gaining awareness through intrapreneurship, cold networking, public speaking, and writing is the first step in the process of building such a network.

The next step is nurturing and cultivating your network to create relationships built on trust. Trust is an outcome of serving your network over time.

It's critical to focus on building your network from the earliest stages of your career. You can't wake up one day and expect to lean on a network of people that you haven't engaged with, and provided value to yourself, and expect any results. Foley & Lardner partner Erika Morabito urges young lawyers to, "Focus on marketing, networking, and business development as much as possible. Every minute you can devote to it, do it."

When it comes to building relationships, less is often more. Your goal should not be a big network, but rather an effective network, regardless of its size. If your network is too big and unwieldy, it will be impossible to achieve the primary objective of active network building, which is to have meaningful and engaged relationships with people who can help you throughout your career. If you have too many loose relationships, then you'll have trouble developing deep ones.

A small network of twenty-five people who are loyal, well-connected, and can make introductions to others as needed, is far more beneficial than a loose network of one hundred to two hundred people who aren't invested in your success. You don't need a large network; you just need a small, strategic one that creates a halo effect of influence around you.

A young lawyer's ultimate success at business development is dependent upon planting seeds for the future through strategic and systematic network building and nurturing. You can accomplish this by:

1. Prioritizing among those in your network

2. Establishing a cadence and rhythm around your outreach

3. Connecting the dots for others in your network

4. Always being on message

PRIORITIZE

Begin by taking inventory of your existing network. Assess your social media contacts, friends, and law school classmates. Take stock of professional colleagues both within and outside of your firm. Identify your twenty to forty highest priority and highest potential relationships. Focus on building a small but powerful network of individuals who can help and support your professional objectives, and who you can help and support as well.

Motivational speaker Jim Rohn believes that, "We are the average of the five people we spend the most time with." The same is true in business. Your success will be determined by the strength of your network.

Deb Knupp is one of the top business development consultants in the legal industry. She is a managing partner with GrowthPlay, which ranked as the twenty-second fastest growing privately held company in the country on the 2017 Inc. 5000 list. She believes that young lawyers need to prioritize network-building from day one. As Deb said, "Winners track with winners."

When it comes to building upon existing relationships, particularly high priority ones, young lawyers need to get out and interact with other people. Powerful networks aren't created through email, phone calls, and social media interaction alone. One of the most worthwhile things that associates can do to strengthen their networks is to leave the office and meet people face-to-face. This takes an investment of time, but personalization pays off in this digital age.

All relationships are not equal. Some are disproportionately valuable. Treat them as such.

Deb describes this approach as the sort "high touch" strategy that associates must employ for their highest priority relationships. There's a time and place for digital communication, but nothing can replace the effectiveness of one-on-one interaction to build authentic, meaningful relationships.

ESTABLISH RHYTHM AND CADENCE

Avoid running hot and cold when it comes to staying in touch with members of your network. Don't allow your level of busyness to dictate your level of engagement. Many lawyers tend to tamp down their marketing, networking, and outreach efforts when things get hot. When things get cold they ramp them back up. According to Deb, a better approach is to build a consistent rhythm and cadence around relationship building.

Proactively and consistently stay in touch with members of your network. Don't just have good intentions about networking and outreach activities. Schedule them in advance on your calendar.

Join alumni, young professional, and bar association groups, but not so many that you can't participate in them in a meaningful way. Prioritize groups that consist of people you consider to be a high priority. Instead of limiting your involvement to attending networking events, take on a leadership role within a group so that you have opportunities to rub shoulders with heavy hitters.

Tim Ferriss has one of the strongest networks in business and media, but when he first moved to San Francisco he knew virtually no one. He describes his time spent volunteering for local organizations shortly after moving to California as key to building his network. One anecdote that he frequently shares in his books and on his podcast is how he worked hard—far harder than others—within a particular organization that he volunteered for. As a result, he stood out to the organization's leaders. This allowed him to take on greater responsibility, including recruiting speakers for the organization's annual event. This allowed him to build relationships with leaders within the organization and influential people he recruited to speak at the organization's events.

As Ferriss and others have demonstrated, taking on a leadership role within an organization is a way to build a strong reputation and network. More work is required to serve as the treasurer of an organization as opposed to merely being a run of the mill member. However, by taking on additional responsibility others will perceive you to be a leader, and you'll expand your opportunities to network with other leaders who can have a significant impact on your professional success. Taking on a leadership role in an organization is also a way to build cadence and rhythm into your networking efforts. As a leader, you'll have roles and responsibilities that you must fulfill. Leadership responsibilities are a form of forced discipline that leads to the consistent efforts required to build a network over time.

Keep in mind that not every interaction with members of your network must be, or even should be, face-to-face, or involve the level of commitment required by assuming a leadership role within an organization. Young lawyers have busy schedules so personal interactions need to be supplemented by other means to stay top of mind.

To build a cadence and rhythm around your outreach, consider using the "1, 1, 100 principle" that I use in my networking efforts. Fifty weeks out of the year, take the time to reach out to two high priority members of your network by making one phone call, sending one short handwritten note, forwarding one relevant article, sending one thoughtful email, or setting up one lunch, coffee, or meeting over drinks.

By keeping up this schedule, which should take no more than one hour per week, you'll have taken one hundred actions to strengthen your network by the end of the year. As you develop the habit of consistently reaching out to members of your network you can increase your activity level. This will lead to increased results.

CONNECT THE DOTS

Deb Knupp believes that one of the best ways to build and strengthen a network is to connect people who can help each other. You may not be in a position to develop business from members of your network at this stage in your career, but that doesn't mean that you can't provide another solution to challenges they face. Connecting the dots for others is a great way to build a powerful network.

For example, even as a young associate you likely have more opportunities than you think to aid and influence the business development initiatives involving members of your network.

Don't ignore emails from colleagues asking for recommendations for local counsel in other jurisdictions. Consider whether a law school classmate at another firm can be of service and make an introduction as appropriate. Be aware of the work being pursued within your firm and evaluate whether you have a relationship that can assist in securing the new business.

When I was a summer associate, I learned that a corporate partner was seeking to form relationships with businesspeople in Europe that could lead to opportunities for mergers and acquisitions work. At the time, my friend's brother was the CEO of a European subsidiary of a large U.S.-based financial institution. I was able to make an introduction that led to an ongoing dialogue between the parties and

I built up goodwill with my colleague by getting the conversation started.

Find ways, no matter how small or seemingly insignificant, to connect dots for members of your network to help them achieve their business objectives. Be useful. Be engaged. Get up from behind your desk and get out into the world. People are accomplishing amazing things outside of the four walls of your office. It's important to get out and meet new people and have new experiences on a consistent basis. This will help you to connect dots and even discover dots that no one else knew existed.

Skadden partner Brian McCarthy encourages young lawyers to look for opportunities to help other professionals they interact with during deals and litigation. "Stay connected and let your counterparts know you've got their back," Brian said. "Be a sounding board for them. Be a resource. If you build relationships with other professionals, they will refer others to you."

Accordingly, before you can expect work to flow to you via referrals, work to make connections for others, both internally and externally, to help them generate work for themselves. When the time comes, your investment in helping others to connect dots will pay dividends in your quest to build a book of business.

BE ON MESSAGE

Over the course of your career, you'll have lots of opportunities to interact with members of your network in professional and social settings. Always be prepared when an opportunity arises. Deb Knupp said, "There's no such thing as just drinks or just lunch." Put another way, never waste an opportunity to plant seeds with members of your network.

You never want to be seen as pushy, manipulative, or overbearing, but you don't want to be perceived as passive either. Be message-ready when strategic messaging is appropriate. Be prepared to say something positive about your firm, your practice, or yourself. Do so in a way that's professional and not boastful, but don't shrink from an opportunity to highlight what makes you, your colleagues, and your firm valuable. The key in striking this balance is preparation. If you know what you want to say, when you'll say it, and how you'll say it before going into an encounter, chances are it will come across as intended.

If you study the way that the best rainmakers in your firm develop business, you'll notice that they likely spend a great deal of time marketing and cross-selling the skills of other lawyers in their firm even if they don't possess the skills themselves. To take advantage of such opportunities, you need to acquire a solid knowledge of the services and solutions your colleagues have to offer, as well as confidence in your colleagues' ability to deliver them.

12

Achieve Client-Focused Clarity in Your Marketing and Communications

---

"Having knowledge but lacking the power to express it clearly is no better than never having any ideas at all."

– PERICLES

Winston Churchill was on the outside looking in at the political power structure in Great Britain in the 1930s. Mired in intra-party squabbles with former political allies, Churchill was left out in the cold when a new government was formed in 1931. By mid-decade, as he was entering his 60s, Churchill was widely regarded as washed up and exiled to the political wilderness.

But as we now know, Churchill was not done; far from it, in fact. By 1939 he was appointed to a cabinet position within the government and in 1940 he became prime minister. It was an astonishing turnaround from political outsider to the heights of power.

So how did Churchill engineer this amazing feat?

For one, he saw something that many others did not, which was the increasingly grave threat posed by Nazi Germany to Great Britain, Europe, and the world more broadly. Conventional wisdom at the time, at least among the political power structure, was that accommodation and negotiation were necessary to deal with the Nazis. Churchill thought otherwise. Throughout his time out of power he urged resistance and confrontation, not appeasement. His stance was neither popular nor perceived as viable—until it was. His foresight about the Nazi threat ultimately brought him back to power and helped cement his enduring legacy as a brilliant wartime leader.

But it wasn't just his firm stance on the issues that mattered. While there were other "warmongers" (a term often used to describe Churchill during his political exile) in Great Britain, none were as effective in getting their message across. Churchill had a platform from which to spread his message and unmatched writing and oratorical skills that allowed his message to resonate with people around the world. He cultivated these skills throughout this life. He was a prolific writer and speaker from a young age. He relentlessly practiced and improved his communication skills during his career. He shifted public opinion in the 1930s by writing hundreds of articles and delivering hundreds of speeches.

Churchill is an excellent example of someone who achieved great success by building a powerful personal brand. We can learn a great deal about personal branding by studying and following Churchill's approach to leadership, persuasion, and communication. The means of communication have changed considerably over the years but the fundamental principles upon which a strong reputation and a powerful personal brand are built have not. The steps Churchill took to regain popularity and loyalty among his constituents during the first half of the twentieth-century in Great Britain are virtually the same as those required to build a strong personal brand today.

First, he identified a niche that he was passionate and knowledgeable about. He beat the drum relentlessly, and almost exclusively, about the Nazi threat for nearly a decade. In today's parlance, the press would refer to Churchill as a "one issue" politician. When people thought of Churchill during this period, they thought of his strong stance against what he perceived as a growing threat. He was proven correct and built up enormous career capital as a result.

Second, he used the tools at his disposal to spread the word about the dangers posed by Nazism, both in Great Britain and around the world. He didn't start speaking and writing when he was out of power. He honed these skills throughout his lifetime. Accordingly, when his message mattered he was ready to deliver it forcefully and convincingly. Because he had already built a platform, he had a means to speak directly to his audience.

Third, through his speaking and writing during the 1930s, he established trust and credibility. This didn't happen quickly. It took many years in the "wilderness" before his message landed. He didn't move toward public opinion; it moved toward him. He earned hard-won respect, then power, and he was able to wield that power effectively because he had built up a bank account of reputational capital. He stuck to his message when it was unpopular so people had confidence that he would carry through on it once it became popular.

The rest is history, and the key lesson we can draw from Churchill's example is: When it comes to building your personal brand, it's critical that the story you're trying to tell is clear, simple, and focused on your audience's needs and interests. There are several reasons for this, and one of the most important is the issue of self-interest—that is, the self-interest of members of your audience, not your own.

In 1943, psychologist Abraham Maslow published a paper called

"A Theory of Human Motivation," in which he argued that all humans have certain basic needs and that these needs are hierarchical. His theory is known as "Maslow's Hierarchy of Needs."

Maslow argued that our primary motivation as a species is to survive. As a result, we are always on the lookout for information that enables our survival. Further up the hierarchy are needs related to our desire to thrive. We want to survive and thrive, and so we're very discerning about the information we digest.

From commercials and emails to Facebook and Instagram posts, we're bombarded by thousands of messages every day. We tune most of them out because they don't further our self-interest. It's a survival mechanism with primal roots. Our ancestors had to worry about a predator jumping out from behind a bush so they had to be on the lookout for danger while walking along a trail. Our approach to scanning for information is much the same today. We have limited mental bandwidth so we pick and choose what to pay attention to based on our self-interest.

Communicate to me in a way that reveals your obvious motivation to make money for yourself, and I'll ignore you. But explain to me how you can help me make money? Now we're talking. When it comes to crafting a compelling message, it's incumbent upon the messenger to take these motivations into account.

The problem is, when faced with the challenge of selling ourselves, we tend to talk and write about *what we care about*. After all, we're motivated by the same self-interest as our audience. We want to talk about *what matters to us* but members of our audience want to hear about *what matters to them*. This causes a disconnect in most brand messaging which prevents ideas from breaking through.

Instead of crafting a brand message that is clear, simple, and focused on client needs and interests, most lawyers do the opposite. They communicate a muddled, complicated, and self-interested message full of platitudes that are meaningless to clients. They speak in generalities using jargon because they are afraid of turning someone off, and as a result they never turn anyone on. Clients don't care what law school you attended or what awards you've won. They want to know how you can help them to survive and thrive. They don't care if you're a superstar lawyer. They want to achieve a super result. Clients want to associate with lawyers who speak their language, which is the language of business, and more specifically *the language of their business.*

Clients aren't motivated to buy legal services; they're trying to buy outcomes. Accordingly, from your website biography and your LinkedIn profile to your blog posts and elevator pitch, begin with an understanding of who you're communicating with and what matters most to them.

Clients want to hire a lawyer who understands and empathizes with them. If you can communicate in a way that makes clear that you know what it's like to walk in your clients' shoes, they'll feel understood and trust you to solve their problems. In every interaction with a client, prospective client, colleague, or referral source, lead with understanding and empathy then demonstrate expertise and authority.

This is the reason to have a niche and why identifying your niche is the first step in the process of building a powerful personal brand. You need to know who it is that you serve before you can have a meaningful and contextualized conversation with them. By steeping yourself in an industry niche, you'll have a deeper understanding of the challenges and opportunities facing decision makers within the space and you can speak their language. Having a niche allows you to craft a tight, relevant message to a specific audience rather than an overly broad, unduly complex, and watered down message to a wide audience. This builds trust with those you're trying to reach.

Churchill had success branding himself as a capable wartime leader because he understood the angst of his audience and spent a decade hammering home his message. He did so in a way that appealed to his audience's self-interest. He painted a picture that allowed people to understand and appreciate that if they followed his lead, they would be safe from the evil forces lurking beyond Great Britain's shores. The people of Great Britain wanted to survive. When the risks became acute they were ready to listen to Churchill and his message of security through strength.

Keep this principle in mind throughout your career: **The best way to create meaningful awareness of your personal brand is to focus all of your efforts on fulfilling the needs and desires of the market you hope to serve.**

Discomfort is the Way

I started my legal career on September 17, 2001. I was supposed to be a mergers and acquisitions lawyer, but after the 9/11 terrorist attacks I was shifted to the corporate restructuring group. Planes were grounded and financial markets closed. The economy was still reeling from the dot-com crash. No one knew what was going to happen, and companies were putting contingency plans into place, which in many cases meant preparing for Chapter 11 bankruptcy.

It was intense and I was unprepared. This was my first real job. I had not taken a single class in law school about bankruptcy law and everyone in the group was so busy that there were few opportunities to ask questions or get feedback. It was trial by fire.

The next four months were a blur of all-nighters and overwhelm. I had too much work and most of it was way beyond what I was capable of, or at least what I thought I was capable of, at the time.

It took everything I had to keep my head above water and my wits about me, which meant I had nothing left for anyone or anything else. I was newly married. We were living in a new city and had not made many friends yet. My wife had just started a new job with 9 to 5 hours.

I was rarely home. When I was home I wasn't. I may have been physically present but not mentally or emotionally so. I'd come home, crash, and do it all over again. A couple of months in, and more than $100,000 in debt from law school loans, and I was questioning my career choice. There were times that I fantasized about walking away to teach or do something—*anything*—to escape my circumstances. We were struggling as a couple. I kept telling my wife that things would get better but I didn't know that to be true.

Eventually they did. The world and the markets calmed down and things took on a more manageable cadence at work. I got my head back above water. Things started clicking. I settled into a routine. I learned how to approach and solve problems. I became more organized and productive. I became a better lawyer.

At the same time, I made lots of mistakes along the way. One of the biggest was not stopping from time to time to understand and appreciate the progress I was making. I'd move closer to my goals but each new stage I reached became the new normal and I'd move on to the next goal. I was moving ahead but it didn't feel that way.

In the moment, it's easy to fixate only on your struggles and failures if you never look back at how far you've come. If you take the time to look back, you'll realize that the good things didn't happen despite the bad ones, they happened because of them. Put another way, the only way to succeed is to fail.

As a lawyer, developing a tolerance for failure—which, for purposes of this discussion, let's define as "failure to live up to your, or someone else's, high expectations"—is critically important. If you fail it means you tried. And you can't win without trying.

Michael Jordan is one of the greatest basketball players of all time. The only way he made lots of shots is because he took lots of shots (and missed a significant percentage of them). In 1923, Babe Ruth set records for the most home runs and highest batting average in a season. He also set the record for most strikeouts. If you want to hit the ball you need to swing. Sometimes you'll miss. Similarly, the only way you can learn to take a good deposition is to take a bad one. Failing provides valuable feedback that can be applied when you try again—and win. Success, therefore, is a byproduct of failure. As Robert F. Kennedy said, "Only those who dare to fail greatly can ever achieve greatly."

Failing is a skill to be trained and refined. And as with any skill, practice makes perfect. This gets to the core of what makes the practice of law both frustrating and exhilarating. To get better at it you need to stretch yourself. To grow you need to change. And to change you need to grow.

Growth involves a great deal of discomfort at times. For example, to create awareness of your personal brand, you need to put yourself in positions to get noticed—in the front of the room, on the other end of the phone, behind the microphone, and at the top of an article with your byline exposed for all to see. You have to get comfortable with being front and center, and for most of us that's a place that feels pretty uncomfortable.

Your approach to your career comes down to a choice between two paths. One feels safe, the other feels fraught with risk. One requires conformity, the other originality. One leads away from fear, the other straight toward it. One feels comfortable—but discomfort is the way.

Those who follow the path toward change are not fearless. In fact, they often feel fear more acutely than those who choose to walk a more well-trod path. But they don't run from the fear, they dance with it. Fear is not a barrier; it's what drives them.

In other words, Essential Associates who train themselves to become more resilient and accountable, and take the steps necessary to build books of business by putting their thought leadership into the marketplace of ideas, experience nervousness and anxiety, too. They just push through the fear. They start to use fear as a compass to guide them rather than perceiving it as an obstacle to avoid.

Fear stops us from doing many things, such as having the courage to define who we are as a lawyers, advocating for what we have to offer, and making progress on ambitious goals. We tell ourselves that we will take action "when the time is right." But then years pass, and we're still facing the same circumstances in our careers, despite an intense desire for change and growth.

The truth is that the only time that is ever right is *right now*. The activities you'll have to engage in to become a leader and develop business as a lawyer, such as writing, public speaking, and networking can be scary at times. Waiting for the fear to go away is a hopeless strategy. It never will. At some point, you have to be more afraid of settling for mediocrity than you are of chasing your dreams and failing.

It takes courage to face the fear and move toward it. But the more you face it the more it becomes a habit. You learn that taking the plunge is not as scary as you thought so you leap again. And again. Pretty soon, you can't help but stretch yourself in new and exciting ways.

Soon you'll come to realize that fear is not something to avoid; it's something to embrace. You'll see and feel the progress you're making, not despite the fear, but because of it. You'll grab fear by the throat and never let go. Instead of avoiding speaking and networking opportunities, you'll seek them out. You won't shrink from tough assignments, you'll raise your hand.

Great success as a lawyer is within your grasp. You know what you need to do. You understand what it takes. You just need to summon the courage and conviction to do it.

Think big because nothing is stopping you from achieving extraordinary results. Take the first step. Then another. Pretty soon the angst and doubt that clouded your first few years as a lawyer will be a distant memory. You'll gain confidence, become more passionate, and the road before you will become broader and smoother. There will still be obstacles—there always are—but your past experiences will allow you to navigate them more easily.

The life of a lawyer is not for everybody. It requires hard work, discipline, and an uncommon commitment to excellence. Unlike in most professions, you're not just fighting an internal battle within a vacuum. There's an adversary on the other side looking to exploit every mistake and ill-conceived move you make. This means that successful lawyers must not only make an uncommon commitment to excellence but have uncommon courage as well.

If you can rise above the challenges you're facing, you'll find, as many before you have, that the profession you have chosen can be one that is deeply satisfying and meaningful. It can provide both professional fulfillment and financial security. But success as a lawyer doesn't happen by accident. It requires a career-long commitment that starts the day you step foot in your firm. It's there for the taking. But it's not a gift, and no one is entitled to it—it's a hard-won reward.

The successful lawyers who shared their wisdom and insights in this book wouldn't have wasted their time if they didn't believe in your potential to become a great lawyer. They believe in you. Your firm believes in you—you wouldn't be where you are if that was not the case. Now that you understand what it takes to become an Essential Associate, I hope you believe in yourself, too.

The road to mastery is long. But now that you know the way the journey should feel a whole lot less uncertain. You know what it takes. *You have what it takes.* Just take the first step. Then the next. After that, you'll be on your way.

RESURCES

Free Resources

Several free resources are available on my website that will help you learn more about what it takes to build your personal brand, and lay the foundation for future business development. Visit **www.hcommunications.biz/books** to download:

How to Make an Impact on LinkedIn:
A Step-by-Step Guide for Lawyers

Learn the essential steps to build a network, brand,
and book of business using LinkedIn.

Personal Branding for Lawyers:
Self-Assessment Workbook

Gain a deeper understanding of how to assess your
unique strengths and weaknesses as a lawyer.

Join My Monthly Newsletter

Lawyers who succeed over the long-term are lifelong learners. They read, study, remain curious, and put what they learn into action.

Each month I identify and distill what I read (books and articles), listen to (audiobooks and podcasts), and discover (tips and tools) into a short email of recommendations for lawyers and legal marketing professionals. From marketing and personal productivity, to cool gadgets, software, and tools, you'll receive lots of stimulating ideas that will inform and inspire you.

Visit **www.hcommunications.biz/newsletter** to sign up, or you can just send me an email at jay@hcommunications.biz and tell me you want to receive the email (just put Resource List in the subject line).

ADDITIONAL RESOURCES

90-Day Personal Brand Building Road Map

To help you take action on the ideas addressed in Part Two of this book, I created the "90-Day Personal Brand Building Road Map," which is available to purchase and download on my website at www.TheEssentialAssociate.com and www.attorneyatwork.com/law-practice-books.

The 90-Day Road Map will help you identify weaknesses and showcase strengths so that you can effectively project your personal brand to the marketplace. It builds on the lessons taught in this book and will help you to both create and implement a plan to build your brand. The ninety-day timeframe is not to suggest that building a personal brand takes ninety days. The truth is you never stop building a brand. The purpose is to get you moving and racking up small wins so that you have the momentum to keep moving forward.

The Essential Associate Academy

Want to go even deeper and accelerate your progress toward becoming an Essential Associate?

In October 2018 (and every October thereafter), I will be launching The Essential Associate Academy, which is an online training program that teaches young lawyers in their first or second year of practice how to excel at legal marketing, business development, and personal brand building. It also addresses how young lawyers can gain strength in the Five Characteristics necessary to achieve success in the practice of law. The program prioritizes strategic planning and being action-oriented, and includes elements to ensure accountability.

The Essential Associate Academy takes place over a six-month period, and involves live webinar training sessions taught by top experts in the fields of productivity, personal branding, business development, writing, public speaking, and more. Live training sessions are supplemented by exclusive content, live webinar Q&A sessions, instructional guides, and a private online community in which to share insights and information, and interact with peers in the profession.

Are you doing what is necessary on a consistent basis to become a successful lawyer in today's competitive marketplace? Would instruction, coaching, and accountability from a team of leading experts help you to stay on track? If so, consider registering for The Essential Associate Academy, a dynamic learning environment for growth-minded young lawyers.

Making a small investment now to learn what it takes to succeed in both the practice of law and the business of law will pay big dividends down the road. To learn more about The Essential Associate Academy, and to be notified when registration opens (which is expected to be in July 2018, and every July after that), visit **www.TheEssentialAssociate.com.**

ABOUT JAY HARRINGTON

For the last decade, I have devoted myself to helping lawyers and law firms build stronger brands and bigger books of business by providing them consulting and creative services, coaching, and group training.

Marketing and Business Development Consulting for Law Firms

I am a co-founder and chief strategist at Harrington, one of the country's leading marketing and creative services agencies. At Harrington, we help law firms of all sizes achieve clarity and client-centric focus in their marketing and build stronger brands, better websites, and larger books of business in the process. In the noisy and ultra-competitive environment in which law firms compete, a law firm's marketing must meet clients where they are, which is online, in control, and searching for a story that resonates.

225

Attorney Coaching

I am an executive coach who blends strategic consulting and problem-solving counseling to help lawyers set and reach their business objectives. I work with lawyers to identify and assess their goals, and then devise strategic action plans to achieve them. After goals are defined then action plans are put in place. My most important job as a coach is to hold clients accountable to the goals they set. Lawyers have the solutions to the challenges they face within them. I just help them to unlock their potential and set a course for success.

Speaking and Workshops for Groups of Attorneys

I specialize in attorney business development training for law firms, both big and small. My presentations and workshops emphasize the importance of smart strategy, action, and accountability, and cover topics related to legal marketing and business development, including:

- Personal Branding for Lawyers
- Building a Niche Practice
- Generating New Business Through LinkedIn
- Building a Powerful Network

I tailor my talks and training sessions to meet client objectives, and I adjust my approach based on the experience level—from junior associate to senior partner—of my audience. My goal is to leave attorneys educated, energized, and inspired to tackle new challenges.

Interested in working with me? Learn more by contacting me at **jay@hcommunications.biz,** 313-432-0287, or visit my agency website at **www.hcommunications.biz**.

About Me

I am an attorney, author, public speaker, executive coach, and marketing consultant. This is my second book (third if you count the children's picture book I wrote and published in 2017). My first business non-fiction book, *One of a Kind: A Proven Path to a Profitable Law Practice*, was published by Attorney at Work in 2016. In addition to my writing and consulting, I frequently speak at law firm training sessions and retreats, bar association gatherings, and other industry events on topics related to personal branding and business development.

Previously, I was a commercial litigator and corporate bankruptcy attorney at Skadden, Arps, Slate, Meagher & Flom in Chicago, and Foley & Lardner in Detroit. I also co-founded a boutique corporate bankruptcy firm in metro Detroit in 2009, which focused on automotive restructuring work. I earned my law degree from the University of Michigan Law School in 2001 and played baseball (and, yes, studied) at Bowling Green State University. I had the good fortune of competing in the College World Series regional tournament in 1998 (although we were knocked out by the number one-ranked University of Miami Hurricanes).

You can read more of my writing on my blog. Please visit **www.simplystatedblog.com** to subscribe. I look forward to continuing this conversation with you!

ADDITIONAL INSIGHTS FROM ATTORNEYS AND OTHER PROFESSIONALS

This book could easily have been one hundred pages longer. During my research, I received so much great advice from so many different people that it was a real challenge to synthesize it down to a manageable length. What follows is additional wisdom from lawyers and other professionals who have important things to say to young lawyers about what it takes to become successful.

*****

Practice with perspective. Your career is very important, but it's not more important than your spouse, your children, your family, or your soul. Stay true to yourself, your personality, and your moral compass. Practice with integrity. If you're discouraged or have anxiety about an argument, about opposing counsel, or about a case, use it as fuel to research more, learn more, and prepare better. If you're overwhelmed with a particular case, client, or type of law, ask senior partners for help, talk to your peers, and learn to say NO to certain types of cases. If you can learn to say NO, your career can be much more fun!

Doug Bailey, Bailey|Stock|Harmon|Cottam LLP

*****

I'm now in my forty-seventh year of "practices." Love what you are doing and be open to making changes when opportunities present themselves. I said "practices" because there will be opportunities to make changes and to grow. While in school get out of school and volunteer or work in offices and with people you admire and with potential long-term interest. Once out of school join and get active in bar activities. Contribute and put in the extra time.

However, pick activities that interest you. Before you know it, you will be chairing the committee, speaking on a topic, and writing articles. These are decent and honorable ways to contribute and to get known. Referrals will flow from fellow attorneys who respect your integrity and work ethic. Older lawyers want to know younger lawyers, so make friends by offering to join in a cause that interests you. Again, don't just join, but contribute. My path has been motivated by trying to be helpful, honest, and competent. Approach law as an honorable profession and it will reward you.

Martin Reisig, Reisig Mediation

*****

If I had to pick one priority to focus on, it would be the need to realize that a young lawyer must be passionate about what they do. They must love what they do, but they must also realize they should take care with "loving who they do this for." From day one on the job, they are, in fact, entrepreneurs and must look at themselves as being "self-employed," regardless of whether they work for a huge firm, a smaller firm, or they are in reality on their own. With that comes the importance of branding, brand marketing, business development, and, yes, sales. Lots and lots of sales. They will be faced with selling their higher-ups within their firm on their expertise and their ideas. They must sell their clients on solution alternatives. They must sell the opposing team on their positions, and they must sell judges and juries as well.

Today, selling tends to get a very bad rap. It is often seen as manipulative, or used-car salesman-like. The reality is people don't "buy," they are sold. And the best at this help their referral sources and their clients feel that, indeed, these young lawyers are their optimum and preferred go-to resources. These young folks must complement this with a very disciplined, targeted, and consistent brand building and business development process. You must be able to stand out in a crowd, and the best brand development strategy is to find a niche and implement a strategy of one-to-many in addition to a local area selling strategy. The lawyer must realize they are in the solutions business, and the relationship-building business. They must get out in their communities and touch their referral sources; including lunches, dinners, events, association involvement, and entertainment. Three emails per day, three phone calls per day, and three face-to-face interactions per week, over time when combined with a one-to-many electronic brand development strategy, will be single most important things to do over the course of a career to keep the pipeline of leads continuously flowing.

"Selling," unfortunately, is a dirty word, but each of us in the professional services world has to embrace sales and constantly prioritize its importance, and we must commit to a lifetime of honing these skills if we want to succeed.

Tony Wayne, IronHorse LLC

*****

I would tell any first or second year attorney to figure out what interests them and excites them about the practice of law (area of law, subject matter) and then go find the attorneys who are at the top of the profession in those areas and do everything possible to get a job working for those firms and under those attorneys regardless of the salary they are offering. The best way to become the best is to work for the best and learn how they do it.

Andrew D. Wyman, Esq., Saavedra | Goodwin

*****

Make (and keep) yourself relevant, which requires that you:

- Understand business and business history. Legal service demand derives from business activity, challenges, and opportunities. If you don't understand business, you can't contribute to the ongoing conversation among clients and prospects. If you don't you're irrelevant and unwelcome; a mere vendor. Understanding business history enables you to recognize the signs of industry or company decline, so you can disinvest and pivot to one that's ascendant.

- Read prodigiously and diversely. Not legal stuff, but business stuff, world stuff, science stuff, technology stuff, life stuff. To be interesting, be interested.

- Master marketing and sales. This is the critical skill set. Invest time and your own money to get training and coaching throughout your career.

- Prioritize marketing and sales. Schedule it every week. Otherwise, you'll only do it sporadically, ineffectively, and you'll have little influence over your career and earnings.

- Focus on an industry. Companies rise and fall, but industries endure and evolve. Somebody is always buying something.

That something will change, but your industry knowledge allows you to anticipate it, refocus, and reposition yourself.

- Don't get married to today. You'll likely have twelve job or career changes in your lifetime. Remain aware of change in the world. Don't remain in a declining category of service, firm, or even the law itself.

- Prepare yourself for a solo career. You may not choose that route, but put yourself in a position to generate your own work.

- Avoid debt. Nothing shrinks your options or produces stress like debt.

Mike O'Horo, RainmakerVT

BOOK RECOMMENDATIONS

The purpose of this book is to help you lay a strong foundation for success in your career. Your journey may start here, but it certainly doesn't end here—at least it shouldn't. Accordingly, below is a list of books that I suggest you read to dive even deeper into the key topics and lessons from this book.

Accountability

Extreme Ownership: How U.S. Navy SEALs Lead and Win by Jocko Willink and Leif Babin

Resilience

Rising Strong by Brené Brown

Productivity

The ONE Thing by Gary W. Keller and Jay Papasan

Growth-Mindedness

Mindset: The New Psychology of Success by Carol S. Dweck

Building a Niche Practice

Essentialism: The Disciplined Pursuit of Less by Greg McKeown

Building a Personal Brand

One of a Kind: A Proven Path to a Profitable Law Practice by Jay Harrington (Shameless plug!)

Building a Strong Network

How to Win Friends and Influence People by Dale Carnegie

ACKNOWLEDGMENTS

Writing a book, like building a legal practice, takes a long time and is not an individual endeavor. I would like to express my deepest gratitude to the people who supported me throughout the process.

Thank you, first and foremost, to my family, including my wife Heather and daughters Madison, Emma, and Kinsey, who supported me while I spent many hours hunkered down in my office thinking, researching, and writing.

I'm forever grateful to all of the attorneys, consultants, and other professionals who contributed their insights to the book. Thanks, also, to friends and colleagues who took the time to read drafts and advance copies of the book and provided invaluable feedback, especially David Dragich and Tom Chinonis.

Thank you, everyone, for what you did to help make this book possible!

NOTES

Chapter 1

http://legalsolutions.thomsonreuters.com/law-products/ns/solutions/peer-monitor/report-on-the-state-of-the-legal-market-repository?CID=TRSite

https://www.wsj.com/articles/biz-stone-life-after-twitter-1396045713

http://abovethelaw.com/2016/04/the-5-things-you-must-do-to-make-partner/

https://www.americanbar.org/resources_for_lawyers/profession_statistics.html

https://tim.blog/2016/12/07/testing-the-impossible-17-questions-that-changed-my-life/

http://sethgodin.typepad.com/seths_blog/2017/03/drip-by-drip-and-the-thunderclap.html

Chapter 3

http://fortune.com/2012/10/25/the-best-advice-i-ever-got/

http://time.com/4306492/boost-emotional-resilience/

https://www.nytimes.com/2015/10/26/your-money/learning-to-deal-with-the-imposter-syndrome.html

Chapter 4

http://harvardmagazine.com/2015/12/rhetoric-and-law

http://blog.chron.com/ultimatetexans/2015/01/j-j-watt-rewards-himself-with-log-cabin-in-middle-of-nowhere/#29459101=0

https://www.wsj.com/articles/SB111196625830690477

http://www.heraldscotland.com/news/13164213.Orwell_s_son_to_visit_house_on_Jura_where_1984_was_written/

https://www.nytimes.com/roomfordebate/2014/11/24/you-wont-believe-what-these-people-say-about-click-bait/click-bait-is-a-distracting-affront-to-our-focus

http://calnewport.com/books/deep-work/

http://www.npr.org/2013/05/10/182861382/the-myth-of-multitasking

https://ideas.repec.org/a/eee/jobhdp/v109y2009i2p168-181.html

http://www.economist.com/node/13881008

Chapter 5

https://www.forbes.com/sites/jeenacho/2016/07/30/study-indicates-lawyers-struggling-with-substance-use-and-other-mental-health-issues/#395602b7b854

http://www.abajournal.com/news/article/why_a_career_website_deems_associate_attorney_the_unhappiest_job_in_america/

http://www.pursuit-of-happiness.org/history-of-happiness/mihaly-csikszentmihalyi/

http://citeseerx.ist.psu.edu/viewdoc/download?doi=10.1.1.491.28&rep=rep1&type=pdf

https://unmistakablecreative.com/podcast/the-profound-power-of-personal-commitment-with-kamal-ravikant

Chapter 6

http://www.economist.com/node/14116121

http://sethgodin.typepad.com/seths_blog/2016/07/a-drop-in-the-bucket.html

https://www.careerbliss.com/facts-and-figures/careerbliss-happiest-and-unhappiest-jobs-in-america-2013/

https://www.theatlantic.com/business/archive/2014/07/the-only-job-with-an-industry-devoted-to-helping-people-quit/375199/

https://abovethelaw.com/2017/03/biglaw-associates-offered-worklife-balance-perks-that-go-unused/

https://aasm.org/resources/pdf/pressroom/adult-sleep-duration-consensus.pdf

https://www.fastcompany.com/3057465/why-six-hours-of-sleep-is-as-bad-as-none-at-all

https://biglawbusiness.com/law-firms-promote-flexible-work-arrangements-lawyers-dont-use/

http://fortune.com/2016/11/30/apple-lawyer-amelia-boone-spartan/

http://www.chicagotribune.com/lifestyles/stevens/ct-amelia-boone-obstacle-athlete-balancing-1206-20151206-column.html

https://hbr.org/2011/05/the-power-of-small-wins

Chapter 7

https://www.psychologytoday.com/blog/bouncing-back/201106/the-no-1-contributor-happiness

Chapter 9

http://www.nytimes.com/1993/12/10/news/bar-portrait-scrappy-lawyer-leaves-subject-unflattered-trying-remove-some-warts.html

https://silicongenesis.stanford.edu/transcripts/sonsini.htm

Chapter 10

http://thisweekinstartups.com/chris-sacca-matt-mazzeo-pt2/

https://www.levo.com/posts/6-essential-tips-for-work-and-life-from-warren-buffett

https://www.attorneyatwork.com/fear-of-speaking/

https://abovethelaw.com/2011/12/inside-straight-building-a-practice-a-case-study/

https://www.reddit.com/r/IAmA/comments/34ak5w/i_am_tim_ferriss_author_angel_investor_host_of/

Chapter 12

https://en.wikipedia.org/wiki/Winston_Churchill

http://psychclassics.yorku.ca/Maslow/motivation.htm

Made in United States
Orlando, FL
25 February 2022

15165301R00135